TYLER
FLORENCE

/ DINNER AT
MY PLACE

Meredith Books / Des Moines, IA

Meredith Books
1716 Locust Street
Des Moines, Iowa 50309-3023
meredithbooks.com

Printed in the United States of America.

First Edition.
Library of Congress Control Number: 2008922213
ISBN: 978-0-696-24158-1

For my wife, Tolan, the love of my life. You've created a wonderful place for us to call home. Thanks for getting me out to California and putting up with all of the long hours, messy kitchens, and camera crews. Most importantly, thank you for our two beautiful children, truly your best work. I would do it all over again with you in a second. Until the end, all my love. —TF

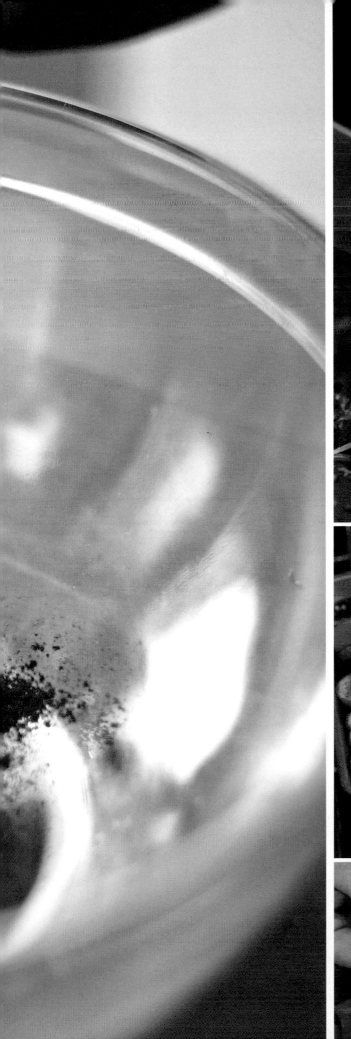

A

COUPLE OF WEEKS AGO, I RAN INTO ONE OF MY NEIGHBORS ON MY MORNING COFFEE RUN, AND WE DECIDED IT WAS ABOUT TIME THAT WE GOT TOGETHER WITH OUR FAMILIES FOR DINNER.

I spend a lot of time on the road doing my thing, and I really enjoy any chance I get to meet the people in my little Northern California town, Mill Valley. Now, I've met this guy before, and he knows what I do for a living, so when the idea of dinner came up, he suggested that I pick my favorite restaurant in town. As is sometimes the case, I blurted out the first thing that came to my mind. "That's easy! The best restaurant in town is my house!" Wow, what a jerk! Who the heck do I think I am? Well, luckily, he knew what I meant, and he didn't cross me off the good neighbor list right off the bat.

Here's what I was trying to communicate: My home is my sanctuary and the kitchen is the nucleus, the lifeblood of my household and my chosen medium of communication with the world. On a daily basis, I express my thoughts, feelings, and emotions through my cooking, and I cannot think of a better way to spend quality time with my family, my friends, my neighbors— or myself. So when I said that my place is the best restaurant in town, I didn't mean to slight my favorite local chefs; I just meant to say that I'd love to have them in my home, where I can share my life with them and vice versa.

So is my house the best restaurant in town? Well, I guess that remains to be seen. But what I can tell you is that my house is the best place to get to know me and see how I put dinner on the table. Restaurant food from a chef's perspective is one thing, but how a chef puts dinner on the table in his own home is another.

Dinner at My Place is not just full of recipes but also full of complete menus for everyday occasions—just as I put them together for my own table. From a birthday dinner for my wife to a rock 'n' roll taco party with old friends. From a game day menu for the guys to a cozy Sunday night by the fire. In *Dinner at My Place*, I've taken the guesswork out of a variety of situations for you so you can make dinner at your place as special as it is at mine.

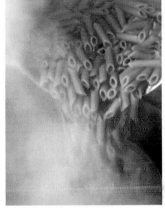

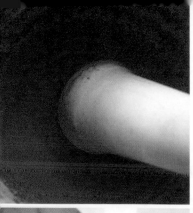

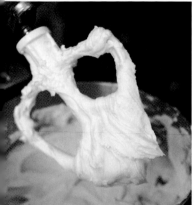

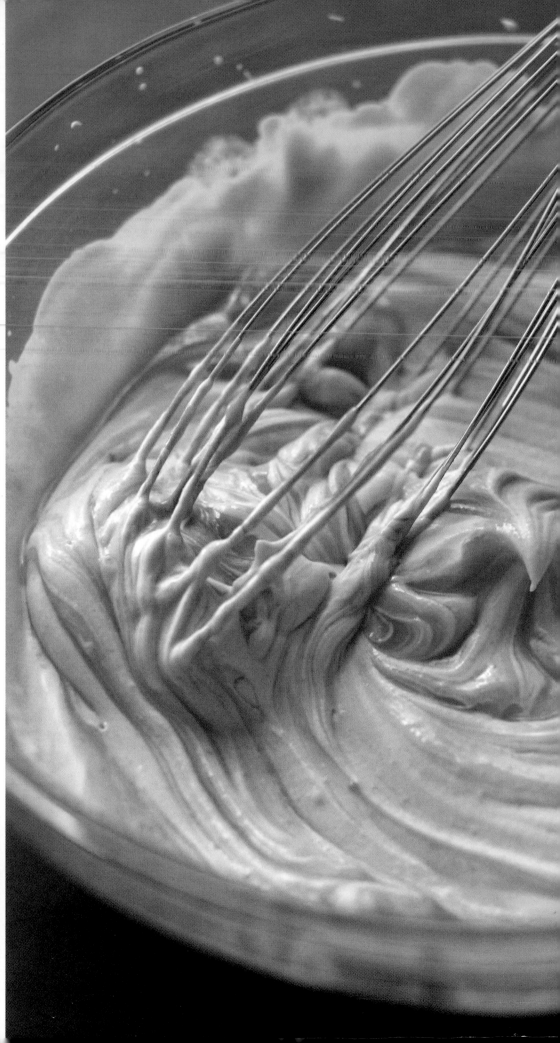

CONTENTS

1 / CRAB SEASON

MENU

> POACHED WEST COAST DUNGENESS CRAB
> DRAWN LEMON BUTTER
> BITTER GREENS SALAD WITH SHAVED
  BEETS AND BALSAMIC
> THE ULTIMATE LASAGNA BOLOGNESE
> FRESH PASTA DOUGH

WHEN I FIRST MOVED TO CALIFORNIA, I WAS TRULY MOVED BY THE SHEER ABUNDANCE OF AMAZING FOOD PRODUCTS AVAILABLE EVERYWHERE.

Meats, fruits, vegetables, wines, cheeses, breads, you name it. If you can eat it, somebody in Northern California is probably producing or raising it to the highest standards of quality for the everyday consumer. For all intents and purposes, the inventive chef Alice Waters created an entire subgenre of cuisine right in her own Northern California backyard. (Google her—she's kind of a big deal!)

With all of this great stuff all around me, it's easy to get spoiled. But sometimes there's something so special and so important to a local culture that you just can't get enough of it. To those of us in the San Francisco Bay Area, the start of Dungeness crab season is one of those things, and it's a great excuse to have some friends over for dinner.

Dungeness crab fishing had a big part in shaping the city of San Francisco, particularly Fisherman's Wharf, when Italian fishermen and Chinatown fishmongers descended upon the wharf to make a living. The Dungeness crab really is the quintessential San Francisco treat (no offense to Rice-A-Roni). In mid-November the waters open up for fishing, and there are crabs everywhere. You can even pitch a net off of a public pier and catch them yourself. At the start of the season, they always seem to be a little bit sweeter and bigger than in the later months, so I love to dive right in and head down to Alioto's on the wharf and pick up some fresh, live beauties for a big crab feed. I look for the liveliest, heaviest, hardest-shelled crabs I can find to make sure I'm getting the freshest and meatiest available. Boil them, clean them, and boom, you're done. It really is that easy.

Crab is indeed a luxury, and I can't get enough of it, but at a dinner party you might want to think about your friends who aren't fans or those who need more of a complete meal. Because Dungeness crab is a winter thing here, I pair it up with a salad of hearty winter greens and a warm, gooey lasagna Bolognese made from scratch. I can't exactly guarantee you that the Sicilian fishermen in the early days of the wharf were eating lasagna with their fresh crab, but this pairing seems to kind of make sense, huh? Either way, I think it's a nice combination, and you end up with a little something for everyone.

As you can see, dinner at my place doesn't need to be a special occasion or a holiday. It can be as simple as enjoying a local tradition with friends. And since my local tradition just happens to include eating some of the greatest seafood delicacies in America, I'm pretty lucky indeed.

POACHED WEST COAST DUNGENESS CRAB | serves 4 to 6 • time: 25 minutes

- 1 Meyer lemon, cut in half
- 10 dried red chiles
- ¼ bunch fresh thyme sprigs (about 4 sprigs)
- 1 garlic head, cut in half through the equator (horizontally)
- 1 tablespoon black peppercorns
- 1 tablespoon kosher salt
- 2 large West Coast Dungeness crabs (about 2 pounds each)

Fill a large stockpot about two-thirds full with water and add lemon, chiles, thyme, garlic, peppercorns, and salt. Set pot over high heat and bring to a boil, then drop in crabs. Reduce heat to a simmer and cook for 12 to 15 minutes. Shut off heat and soak for 5 minutes before straining and cooling. Discard cooking liquid.

To serve, remove cap, cut off gills, and split each crab into 8 pieces. Serve with Drawn Lemon Butter (below).

DRAWN LEMON BUTTER | serves 4 to 6 • time: 9 minutes

- 2 sticks unsalted butter, room temperature
- 1 garlic clove, peeled and gently smashed
- ¼ bunch fresh thyme sprigs (about 4 sprigs)
- 1 lemon, sliced
- 1 teaspoon kosher salt

Put all the ingredients into a saucepan and set over low heat. Slowly melt butter and barely bring to a simmer (the lemon and herbs should become fragrant). Remove from heat and serve warm with Poached West Coast Dungeness Crab (above).

> **IN MID-NOVEMBER THE WATERS OPEN UP FOR FISHING AND THERE ARE CRABS EVERYWHERE. YOU CAN EVEN PITCH A NET OFF OF A PUBLIC PIER AND CATCH THEM YOURSELF.**

AT THE START OF THE SEASON, THEY ALWAYS SEEM TO BE A LITTLE BIT SWEETER AND BIGGER THAN IN THE LATER MONTHS ...

BITTER GREENS SALAD
WITH SHAVED BEETS AND BALSAMIC

serves 4 to 6 • time: 12 minutes

Balsamic Vinaigrette
- 1 shallot, finely diced
- ¼ cup finely chopped fresh Italian flat-leaf parsley
- 1 tablespoon Dijon mustard
- 2 tablespoons balsamic vinegar
- 1 tablespoon sugar
- ¾ cup "O" brand blood orange-infused extra-virgin olive oil*
  Kosher salt and freshly ground black pepper

Salad
- 1 large golden beet
- 1 bunch bitter greens**
- 1 bunch kale**
- ½ bunch beet mizuna**
- ½ head radicchio**
- ½ cup walnuts, toasted
- ¼ pound crumbled goat cheese

Make Balsamic Vinaigrette by combining shallot, parsley, mustard, vinegar, and sugar in a large mixing bowl. To prevent slipping, use a rolled-up kitchen towel to cradle your bowl, then slowly pour in oil in a steady stream as you whisk. Once all the oil has been added and the vinaigrette has emulsified, season it with salt and pepper. Set vinaigrette aside while you prepare the salad.

For salad, peel the beet, then shave it into thin, round slices using a mandoline or sharp knife. Wash and tear the salad greens into bite-size pieces; discard the lower end of any tough stems. Toss greens together with shaved beet and walnuts in a large salad bowl. Dress with Balsamic Vinaigrette. Top with crumbled goat cheese.

*NOTE If blood orange-infused olive oil isn't available, substitute regular extra-virgin olive oil with a splash of blood orange juice.

**NOTE You can substitute your favorite winter salad greens if bitter greens, kale, beet mizuna, or radicchio is not readily available.

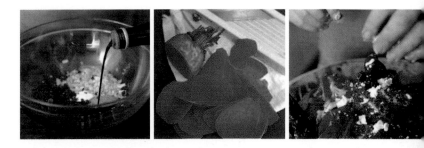

"I love to dive right in and head down to Alioto's on the wharf and pick up some fresh, live beauties for a big crab feed."

THE ULTIMATE
LASAGNA BOLOGNESE | 8 to 10 servings • time: 3 hours 15 minutes *(not including pasta)*

1 recipe Fresh Pasta Dough (see page 27)

Bolognese

2 carrots, cut into large pieces
1 large onion, cut into large pieces
3 ribs celery, cut into large pieces
4 garlic cloves, peeled
4 fresh sage sprigs, leaves only
   Extra-virgin olive oil
1 pound ground beef
1 pound ground pork
   Kosher salt and freshly ground black pepper
2 tablespoons all-purpose flour
1 750-milliliter bottle dry red wine
1 28-ounce can San Marzano whole tomatoes
½ cup whole milk
1 teaspoon ground cinnamon
1 cup grated Parmesan
2 tablespoons finely chopped fresh Italian flat-leaf parsley

Béchamel

2 cups whole milk
3 garlic cloves, peeled
1 bay leaf
1 stick unsalted butter
½ cup all-purpose flour
¼ teaspoon freshly grated nutmeg
   Kosher salt and freshly ground black pepper
1 pound buffalo mozzarella, torn into pieces
¼ cup grated Parmesan
2 tablespoons chopped fresh Italian flat-leaf parsley

Begin by making Fresh Pasta Dough. Follow directions on page 27. After rolling dough through the thinnest setting, hang the sheets of pasta to dry for 20 to 30 minutes.

To make Bolognese, put carrot, onion, celery, garlic, and sage in a food processor and process until you have smooth vegetable pulp. Coat a large, heavy-based pot with oil and set over medium heat. Add vegetable pulp and sauté until fragrant and some of the moisture has evaporated, 4 to 5 minutes. Push the vegetable pulp to one side of the pot. Season ground beef and pork with plenty of salt and pepper, then add to the pot. Stir and break up the meat until it is brown, then dust with 2 tablespoons flour before adding wine, tomatoes, milk, and cinnamon. Bring to a boil, then reduce heat and simmer about 1½ hours, uncovered, until sauce is thick. Add Parmesan and parsley and season with salt and pepper. Set aside while you prepare the Béchamel.

To make the Béchamel, set a large saucepan over medium heat. Add milk, garlic, and bay leaf and bring to a simmer to infuse milk with herb flavors. Set a large saucepan over medium-low heat. Add butter and melt, then sprinkle in flour while you stir with a wooden spoon. Once all of the flour has been combined with the butter, grab a whisk and gradually pour in the herb-infused milk, passing it through a sieve as you go to strain out the aromatics. As the sauce thickens, continue to whisk over low heat, then add nutmeg. Season with salt and pepper and set aside to cool slightly.

Preheat oven to 350°F. To assemble the lasagna, cut the hang-dried pasta sheets to fit a 9×13×3-inch lasagna pan; set the pasta aside. Coat the bottom of the lasagna pan with a thin layer of Béchamel. Top with a layer of lasagna noodles, trimming noodles to fit as necessary. Top the noodle layer with a layer each of Béchamel, Bolognese, and mozzarella pieces. Continue with the layers of lasagna noodles, Béchamel, Bolognese, and mozzarella pieces until you have three complete layers, finishing with mozzarella. Shower the top of the lasagna with Parmesan and parsley. Bake, uncovered, on a tray (to catch the drippings) in the center of the preheated oven for 1 hour. (If the top starts to brown, tent with foil.) Let the lasagna stand for 15 to 20 minutes before cutting.

> **"CRAB IS INDEED A LUXURY, AND I CAN'T GET ENOUGH OF IT. BUT AT A DINNER PARTY YOU MIGHT WANT TO THINK ABOUT YOUR FRIENDS WHO AREN'T FANS OR THOSE WHO NEED A BIT MORE OF A COMPLETE MEAL."**

THE ULTIMATE
LASAGNA BOLOGNESE
(RECIPE, P. 22/23)

FRESH PASTA DOUGH | makes about 1 pound • time: 1 hour 20 minutes *(not including cooking time)*

2 cups all-purpose flour, plus more for dusting
1 teaspoon kosher salt
3 large eggs
2 tablespoons extra-virgin olive oil

Place the 2 cups flour on a clean, flat work surface. Add the salt and mix well with your hands. Shape flour into a mound, then use the side of your hand to scoop out a well in the center. Add the eggs and 1 tablespoon of the oil to the well and beat lightly with a fork. Gradually mix in the flour from the inside wall of the well, using a circular motion. Use one hand for mixing and the other to maintain the shape of the outer wall. Continue to widen the well and incorporate the flour until the dough forms a ball. Using your hands, knead and fold the dough until elastic and smooth; this should take about 10 minutes. Brush the surface with the remaining 1 tablespoon oil and wrap the dough in plastic wrap. Let it rest for 30 minutes.

Cut the pasta dough into 4 chunks. Set aside 1 chunk of dough. Cover the pieces you are not immediately using to prevent them from drying out. Dust the counter and the one piece of dough with a little flour. Roll the chunk of dough through a pasta machine at the widest setting to form a strip. Fold that strip in half, turn it 90 degrees, and roll it through again. Now you have a nice edge. Roll the dough another 2 or 3 times in the same direction, pulling and stretching it with the palm of your hand as it emerges from the rollers. Crank the machine down one setting and roll the dough through 2 or 3 times. Continue tightening the setting (one setting at a time) and rolling 2 or 3 times on each setting until the machine is at the thinnest setting.

Cut pasta into desired shape, such as angel hair, spaghetti, or tagliatelle. Hang pasta to dry for 20 to 30 minutes. To cook pasta, place a large pot of salted water over high heat and bring to a boil. Drop dried pasta into the boiling water and cook until tender, yet firm (al dente), 2 to 3 minutes for angel hair and 5 to 6 minutes for tagliatelle.

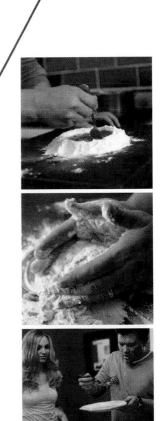

2 / WINNER, WINNER, CHICKEN DINNER

MENU

> ROTISSERIE CHICKEN WITH LEMON, GARLIC, AND FRESH BAY LEAVES
> LEMON ROASTED FINGERLING POTATOES
> WILTED BUTTER LETTUCE, FRESH GARDEN PEAS, AND BEURRE BLANC

THERE'S AN AD ON TELEVISION THESE DAYS STARRING A COUPLE OF MANGY, BEER DRINKIN', NACHO CHEESE CHUGGIN' CHICKENS ON THEIR WAY OUT WEST TO TRY TO PASS THEMSELVES OFF AS REAL CALIFORNIA CHICKENS.

These commercials have turned into a whole series and really are hilarious. But as funny as they may seem, such trickery is not all that far from reality. There have been some great books in the past few years, like *Fast Food Nation* and *The Omnivore's Dilemma,* that have really asked us all to look at what we eat and consider how it affects our bodies and our world. I don't want to get into some kind of preachy manifesto on how the chicken nuggets you ate last night make you a bad person. (Don't worry about it; it's none of my business!) But I do want to talk to you about what you are putting in your body—even if it's just to help you choose the best-tasting chicken you possibly can.

The process our food goes through before it makes it to our tables has sparked a lot of controversy around the world, making us question everything we put in our mouths—from fruit and vegetables to meat and eggs. So unless you know your chicken personally, you're going to have to rely on your local market and the U.S. government to make the best chicken choices. Find a market you trust and ask questions—the more, the better. You'll learn a lot, and your local market may start to pay more attention too. No matter how close you are with your local butcher, remember that he's a salesman and his products are labeled by suppliers who are selling as well. So I'm going to make this simple for you and give you a quick lesson in chicken vocabulary. Listed below are the three most common labels used to identify chicken:

ALL NATURAL You know better than to eat a rubber chicken, right? That's basically what this label promises you—that this chicken is not rubber. The USDA prohibits the use of hormones in raising poultry and most preservatives. But besides that, the chicken can be injected with

just about anything else—from salt-water solutions to seaweed extract—and still be called "all natural." These solutions up your salt intake, change the chicken's flavor, and end up costing you more because they add weight to the chicken. This label just doesn't give you enough to go on.

FREE RANGE Sounds good, right? Vivacious white hens freely roaming sunny, grassy fields with fluffy yellow chicks in tow. Not so much. The USDA allows this label for any chicken that is allowed some access to an outdoor space. Said chicken may never even see that outdoor space, and this designation doesn't address what's out on that yard—the conditions, the food, or the cleanliness. So it's a good start, but free range isn't the be-all and end-all we used to think it was.

CERTIFIED ORGANIC I know there are those of you out there who think that organic is some kind of hippie thing. But get that out of your head and start paying attention to organics—because they're here to stay. The Organic Foods Production Act of 1990 set forth requirements for products labeled as "organic" that ensure your chicken has lived a life dictated by government-mandated standards. It will have been fed only pesticide- and chemical-free feeds of grains and soybeans, not animal byproducts. It also will have lived a life free of antibiotics and medicines. But guess what? It probably wouldn't have needed those antibiotics because organic chickens generally live a life free of the stress and contamination that can make other chickens sick. And of course, all organic chickens are both free range and all natural. See how this works? Whenever I can, I will definitely choose certified organic over the other two options.

So now you know a thing or two about one of America's most popular proteins. While a chicken dinner used to be something pretty special because chickens were expensive, nowadays it's about the most common protein you'll find. Each of us will eat about 90 pounds of it a year! So keep what I've told in you mind but don't leave it at that. Continue your research to formulate your own opinions and decide what you feel comfortable putting in your body. But regardless of whether or not you change your shopping habits to seek out the finest, most-humanely raised organic chickens, I swear to you, we still can be friends.

You've picked your chicken, so let's work on one of the most perfect dishes ever imagined—the roast chicken. This is as simple as it gets. But when done right, it is, without a doubt, as good as it gets!

ROTISSERIE CHICKEN WITH
LEMON, GARLIC, AND FRESH BAY LEAVES | serves 4 to 6 • time: 1 hour

1   5-pound certified organic chicken
    Kosher salt and freshly ground black pepper
1   Meyer lemon, halved
1   garlic head, cut through the equator (horizontally)
4   to 5 fresh bay leaves
½   bunch fresh thyme sprigs (about 8 sprigs)
    Extra-virgin olive oil
1   recipe Lemon Roasted Fingerling Potatoes (see recipe, page 37)
1   recipe Wilted Butter Lettuce, Fresh Garden Peas, and Beurre Blanc
    (see recipe, page 41)

Rinse chicken with cool water and pat dry with paper towels. Season
cavity well with kosher salt and pepper. Stuff cavity with lemon, garlic,
bay leaves, and thyme. Tie bird with kitchen twine and skewer on a
rotisserie rod. Rub outside with oil and season with salt and pepper.

Roast in a rotisserie* about 45 minutes, until golden brown and juices
run clear (180°F). After chicken has roasted for about 15 minutes,
add the Lemon Roasted Fingerling Potatoes under the chicken in
a roasting pan. (Position the pan so the potatoes can catch the
chicken drippings.) Remove chicken and potatoes from the oven.
Tent with foil; let chicken stand for 10 minutes.

Break chicken down into 10 pieces; serve chicken and potatoes with
Wilted Butter Lettuce, Fresh Garden Peas, and Beurre Blanc.

*TIP If you don't have a rotisserie, preheat your oven to 350°F. Place
the Lemon Roasted Fingerling Potatoes (see page 37) in a baking pan.
Place the chicken on top of the potatoes. Roast in preheated oven for
1 hour 30 minutes or until juices run clear (180°F).

> **I KNOW THERE ARE THOSE OF YOU OUT THERE WHO THINK THAT ORGANIC IS SOME KIND OF HIPPIE THING. BUT GET THAT OUT OF YOUR HEAD AND START PAYING ATTENTION TO ORGANICS—BECAUSE THEY'RE HERE TO STAY.**

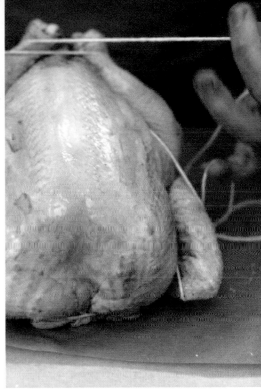

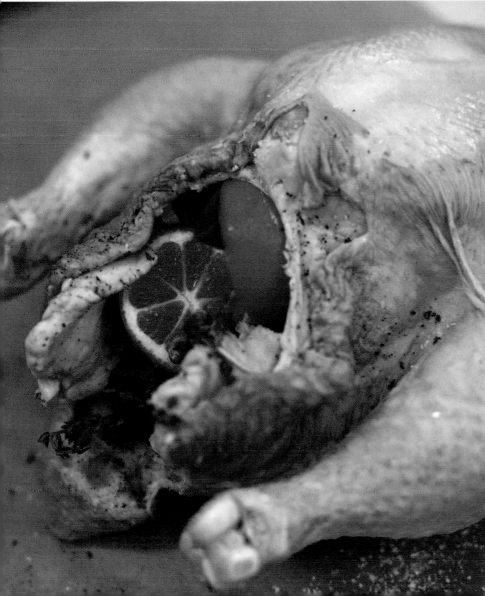
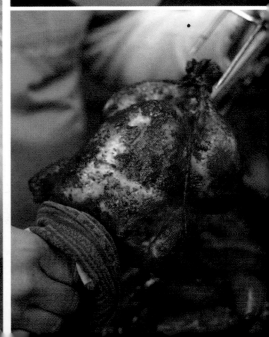

THIS IS AS SIMPLE AS IT GETS. BUT WHEN DONE RIGHT, IT IS, WITHOUT A DOUBT, AS GOOD AS IT GETS!

LEMON ROASTED FINGERLING POTATOES
serves 4 to 6 • time: 35 minutes

2 pounds fingerling potatoes
¼ cup extra-virgin olive oil
1 fresh rosemary sprig, leaves only
2 fresh thyme sprigs, leaves only
1 to 2 Meyer lemons, cut into quarters
Kosher salt and freshly ground black pepper

Wash potatoes and cut lengthwise. Toss potatoes with oil. Toss with rosemary, thyme, and lemon wedges in a roasting pan. Season with salt and pepper, then roast potatoes under the rotisserie chicken for 25 to 30 minutes, until golden brown. (If you don't own a rotisserie, see tip on page 32.) Stir occasionally to coat with chicken drippings and cook evenly. Season once more with salt and pepper before serving.

"While a chicken dinner used to be something pretty special because chickens were expensive, nowadays it's about the most common protein you'll find. Each of us will eat about 90 pounds of it a year!"

WILTED BUTTER LETTUCE, FRESH GARDEN PEAS, AND BEURRE BLANC

serves 4 • time: 25 minutes

Salad
1   large head butter lettuce
1   cup fresh garden peas, blanched in salted water*

Beurre Blanc
1   cup dry white wine
1   shallot, finely chopped
6   black peppercorns
1   bay leaf
½   teaspoon kosher salt
1   stick cold unsalted butter, sliced
    Kosher salt and freshly ground black pepper

For salad, cut off the root of the lettuce and separate leaves. Place the leaves in a large salad bowl with blanched peas.

Just before the chicken and potatoes are done roasting, prepare Beurre Blanc by combining wine, shallot, peppercorns, bay leaf, and the ½ teaspoon salt to a saucepan; place over medium heat. Simmer until sauce is syrupy and just coats the bottom of the pan. Add butter slices, a few at a time, while stirring with a whisk to thicken the sauce and give it a shine. Add salt and pepper to taste. Dress lettuce and peas with some of the warm Beurre Blanc. Toss so the leaves wilt a little.

To serve the complete dish, add the 10 warm chicken pieces (see page 32) and the potatoes (see page 37) to the salad and gently toss to combine. Finish with another drizzle of Beurre Blanc.

*TIP To blanch the peas, submerge them in boiling salted water for about 2 ½ minutes (for fresh peas). Strain them and immediately plunge them into ice water to stop the cooking process. Strain them again and set aside.

3/ TOLAN'S BIRTHDAY DINNER

MENU

> FILET MIGNON WITH BLENDER BÉARNAISE
> BACON AND BRUSSELS SPROUTS HASH
> "BIRTHDAY" CARROT CAKE WITH CREAM CHEESE
  FROSTING AND COINTREAU CARROTS

BIRTHDAYS ARE SPECIAL. YOU'VE HAD ONE EVERY YEAR OF YOUR LIFE, AND WHETHER YOU LIKE IT OR NOT, THEY'RE GOING TO KEEP ON COMIN'.

Even if you stopped counting the candles during the Reagan administration, you still should enjoy your day and treat yourself to (or be treated to) a special dinner. When you were a kid, maybe you enjoyed ice cream and cake served by a clown who looked suspiciously like your grandfather. If you're like me, you're done with the whole pizza party thing. The hot dog thing. The burger bash. Been there, done that. But you're all grown up now, and it's time your birthday dinner caught up.

My wife, Tolan, and I are lucky enough to dine at some of the most amazing restaurants in the world. It's a nice perk in this line of work. But when it comes to our birthdays, we're all about a special meal at home. Now that doesn't mean it's all sweatpants and TV dinners. Sometimes it's nice to have that sexy restaurant experience right at home. You don't have to press the white linens and polish the silver for this one, but I do want you to create a meal that your favorite restaurant would be proud to serve.

With this menu, I've put together Tolan's favorite birthday dinner, and filet mignon is the star. Filet mignon comes from the small end of the beef tenderloin and is the most tender cut of beef. It's also usually the most expensive cut at a restaurant. Not breaking the bank is just another reason to try this one at home.

Despite being very tender, the filet has less fat than, say, a ribeye steak. Accordingly, I like to serve it a little bit more rare than other juicier cuts and incorporate some kind of fat to enhance the flavor. You can wrap it in bacon or top it with a few crumbles of blue cheese, but Tolan's favorite way to top off her filet is with a rich steakhouse classic: béarnaise sauce. Béarnaise can be a challenge, so I've created this version that you can whip up in your blender. Quick, easy, delicious!

Remember, this is a special dinner, so I'm not stopping there. Give the Brussels sprout hash with red pearl onions and crispy bacon a try for something unique and new. It's refined enough to not be overshadowed by the filet, and it plates up beautifully. And at the end of the day, this is still a birthday dinner, grown-up or not, so there's no excuse for skipping the moist and delectable carrot cake.

Forget about the cardboard pizzas and soggy burgers of yesteryear, and don't worry about counting candles or calories. Get dressed up and stay in with this very special birthday menu that will work whenever you want to treat yourself or someone you love.

FILET MIGNON | serves 4 • time: 35 minutes

1   large end piece of beef tenderloin (about 3 pounds), tied and trimmed
    Extra-virgin olive oil
    Kosher salt and freshly ground black pepper
    Assorted fresh herbs (such as thyme, sage, and rosemary)
    Hydroponic watercress (optional)

Preheat oven to 400° F. Drizzle the tenderloin with oil. Season well with plenty of salt and pepper. Sprinkle with assorted fresh herbs. Allow the tenderloin to come to room temperature before cooking. Place a large cast-iron skillet over medium-high heat and sear tenderloin on all sides (add additional oil, if necessary). Place the skillet in the preheated oven and roast the tenderloin for about 15 to 17 minutes. (At this point, a meat thermometer inserted into the thickest part of the meat should read 135°F for medium rare; for medium, roast for 3 minutes more.) Remove from the oven. Tent tenderloin with foil; allow to rest for 10 minutes before slicing. Serve with Blender Béarnaise (see below). If you like, garnish with watercress.

BLENDER BÉARNAISE | serves 4 • time: 15 minutes

¼   cup champagne vinegar
¼   cup dry white wine
2   shallots, minced
3   tablespoons fresh tarragon leaves
3   egg yolks
1   stick unsalted butter, melted
    Kosher salt and freshly ground black pepper to taste

To make the reduction for the béarnaise sauce, combine vinegar, wine, shallot, and half of the tarragon in a small saucepan and place over medium-high heat. Bring to a simmer and cook until reduced by half. Remove from heat and set aside to cool. Blend yolks and béarnaise reduction together in a blender on low speed until combined. With the blender running on medium speed, add one-third of the butter in a slow, steady stream. Once the mixture emulsifies (it will become thick and satiny), turn the blender speed up to high and add the remaining butter. Add the remaining tarragon, season with salt and pepper, and pulse in the blender. Transfer to a dish; hold in a warm spot until ready to serve.

BACON AND BRUSSELS SPROUTS HASH

serves 4 to 6 • time: 25 minutes

Extra-virgin olive oil
4 slices thick cut bacon
4 fresh thyme sprigs
1 pound fingerling potatoes, cut lengthwise
2 cups Brussels sprouts, cut into thick slices
½ pound red pearl onions, peeled and cut in half
Kosher salt and freshly ground black pepper
½ cup reduced-sodium chicken broth
2 tablespoons balsamic vinegar
¼ bunch fresh Italian flat-leaf parsley (4 sprigs), roughly chopped

Set a large sauté pan over medium heat and add a 2-count of oil (about 2 tablespoons). Cut bacon into long, thin strips and add to pan with thyme. Cook for 5 to 7 minutes to render the fat. Remove bacon with a slotted spoon and set aside. Discard half of the fat in the pan. To the remaining fat in the pan, add the potatoes, Brussels sprouts, and onions. Season with salt and pepper and cook until slightly browned. Add chicken broth and continue to cook for 3 to 5 minutes, until liquid has evaporated and vegetables are tender. Remove and discard thyme sprigs. Add vinegar and toss to coat. Cook until vinegar has reduced, then fold in parsley and reserved bacon.

AND AT THE END OF THE DAY, THIS IS STILL A BIRTHDAY DINNER, GROWN-UP OR NOT, SO THERE'S NO EXCUSE FOR SKIPPING THE MOIST AND DELECTABLE CARROT CAKE.

"BIRTHDAY" CARROT CAKE WITH CREAM CHEESE FROSTING AND COINTREAU CARROTS (RECIPE, P. 52/53)

"BIRTHDAY" CARROT CAKE | 1 large cake (serves 8 to 10) • time: 1 hour 45 minutes

1½	cups finely minced carrot
½	cup crushed pineapple, drained
¾	cup finely chopped walnuts
2½	cups all-purpose flour
1	teaspoon baking powder
1	teaspoon baking soda
⅛	teaspoon ground cinnamon
¼	teaspoon ground allspice
¼	teaspoon freshly ground nutmeg
	Pinch kosher salt
1	cup buttermilk
¼	cup molasses
4	large eggs
¾	cup vegetable oil
1½	cups packed dark brown sugar
1	recipe Cream Cheese Frosting (see page 53)
1	recipe Conintreau Carrots (see page 53)

Preheat oven to 375°F. Grease a jelly-roll pan (15×10×1-inch) and line with parchment paper. Set aside.

Combine carrot, pineapple, and walnuts in a medium bowl. Set aside. Mix together flour, baking powder, baking soda, spices, and salt in a large mixing bowl. Mix together buttermilk, molasses, eggs, oil, and dark brown sugar in a separate medium bowl.

Now add the buttermilk mixture to the flour mixture and stir with a wooden spoon to make a batter, then fold in the carrot mixture. Pour into the prepared pan and bake in the preheated oven for 25 to 30 minutes, until cake is set and springs back when gently pressed in the middle. Remove the pan from the oven and allow cake to cool on a rack while you prepare the Cream Cheese Frosting and Cointreau Carrots.

Once the cake has cooled, carefully remove cake from pan. Cut into three equal-size rectangles by cutting the cake crosswise twice. Stack the cake into three tiers with Cream Cheese Frosting in between each layer. Frost the outside of the entire finished cake, smoothing off the edges and corners (an offset spatula works well). Top with Cointreau Carrots and drizzle a little of their syrup on top.

CREAM CHEESE FROSTING

2 pounds cream cheese, room temperature
2 sticks unsalted butter, room temperature
2 cups powdered sugar
1 teaspoon vanilla extract
1 teaspoon lemon zest

Using a standing mixer, beat cream cheese and butter in a large
mixing bowl until it is blended and has a smooth, light texture. Add
the powdered sugar, vanilla, and lemon zest and beat until combined.
Continue to beat until smooth and glossy, about 7 minutes.

COINTREAU CARROTS

1 medium carrot
½ stick unsalted butter
2 tablespoons sugar
¼ cup Cointreau
  Pinch kosher salt

Slice carrot into thin rounds. Put carrot, butter, sugar, Cointreau,
and salt in a small saucepan and place over medium heat. Bring to
a simmer and reduce until carrots are tender and mixture is syrupy,
about 5 minutes.

4

GUYS' GAME NIGHT

N

OW DON'T GET ME WRONG—ABOVE ALL ELSE, I AM A FAMILY MAN. I HAVE A GORGEOUS HOME, THREE BEAUTIFUL KIDS, AND A LOVING WIFE.

But let's not forget that before all of that, the only hint of domestication in my life was my dog, Jake. Family life couldn't be treating me better, but sometimes I just want to have the boys over for some good food and a few laughs.

I had the guys over not too long ago to watch a Golden State Warriors game, and I wanted to put together a menu that was both appropriate for the occasion and unique. A lot of the time, particularly when it comes to watching sports, we get stuck eating the same old things—cardboard nachos with squeeze cheese, faux guacamole, and rubbery, too-hot-to-eat chicken wings. I decided that I wanted to give them something familiar yet new and exciting. When it comes down to it, most guys like chili on game day, so I thought that would be a good starting point.

Chili has a history like no other food, from its roots as a Texas prison staple to today's delicacy of the stars at Hollywood's famous Chasen's restaurant. One of the most popular accounts of chili's humble origins dates back to the mid-1800s, when Texas prisons began serving a cheap stew of beef and chiles instead of the typical gruel of bread and water. The tough meat was cooked down to an edible consistency and mixed with chiles and spices. Soon prisoners and the institutions alike began to take pride in their particular versions, and the various recipes began to live beyond the prison walls. It also has been said that chili began as a frontier food that cowboys ate on their long rides between Texas and the California gold country. I don't really care which version of the story you choose to believe, but I do care that you know one thing: Chili comes from Texas and Texas chili has no beans.

My Prime Rib Chili stays true to its roots, but it's upscale enough to serve to my buddies and Hollywood royalty alike. Because we aren't in prison and I have my choice of ingredients, I upgrade this chili with prime rib, braising it until it falls apart. It's tender and breaks down to a beautiful consistency. To complement the chili, I've created a fresh and moist corn pudding. The sweet potato chips are easy to fry up and a perfect vehicle for the blue cheese dip. Guys are creatures of habit, and when it comes to cooking for the big game or any other guy-centric occasion, you'll win them over by taking the familiar and presenting it in new and exciting ways.

PRIME RIB CHILI | serves 4 to 6 • time: 3 hours

3 pounds cubed beef prime rib
Kosher salt and freshly ground black pepper
Extra-virgin olive oil
2 onions, diced
10 garlic cloves, peeled and halved
3 canned chipotle peppers in adobo, chopped*
1 Jalapeño, seeded and chopped
½ cup Chili Powder (see recipe, below)
2 tablespoons tomato paste
1 28-ounce can whole San Marzano tomatoes
1 tablespoon grated unsweetened chocolate
¼ cup masa harina (tortilla flour)
1 lime, cut into wedges for garnish
Cilantro leaves, for garnish

Season the beef cubes with plenty of salt and black pepper. Set a large, heavy-based pot over medium-high heat and add a 3-count of olive oil (about 3 tablespoons). When the pot is very hot, add the beef and stir until brown. Mix in the onion, garlic, chipotle, and jalapeño, then stir in the Chili Powder. Add tomato paste and pour the entire can of tomatoes with their liquid into the pot; crush tomatoes with the back of a wooden spoon. Stir in chocolate. Add enough water to just cover the meat and simmer, uncovered, until the meat is fork-tender and comes apart with no resistance, about 2 hours. When done cooking, use a wooden spoon and beat the chili vigorously so the meat comes apart in shreds. Thicken the mixture by stirring in the masa harina. Season with salt and black pepper and simmer for another 30 minutes, stirring occasionally. Garnish with lime wedges and cilantro and serve with Corn Pudding with Poblano (see page 65).

CHILI POWDER Seed and hand-tear 2 ancho chiles. Toast chile pieces and 2 tablespoons whole coriander seeds in a dry skillet over low heat until fragrant, shaking the skillet so they don't scorch. Put the chiles and coriander seeds in a blender and pulse until you have a fine powder. Add 2 tablespoons purchased chili powder, 2 tablespoons sweet paprika, 1 tablespoon ground cumin, 1 tablespoon dried oregano, 1 tablespoon sugar, and ¼ teaspoon ground cinnamon. Process until well combined and you have a fine powder. Stir in 2 tablespoons kosher salt. Store in an airtight container for up to 4 months. Makes ½ cup.

*TIP Because hot chile peppers contain volatile oils that can burn your skin and eyes, wear plastic or rubber gloves when handling them. If you do touch the chiles, wash your hands well with soap and water.

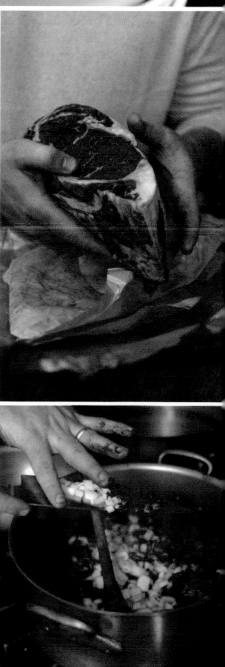

"Because we aren't in prison and I have my choice of ingredients, I upgraded this chili with prime rib, braising it until it falls apart."

CORN PUDDING WITH POBLANO

serves 4 to 6 • time: 1 hour

6 ears fresh corn
1 pint whole milk
1 pint heavy whipping cream
2 cloves garlic, peeled and gently smashed
2 fresh thyme sprigs
2 tablespoons unsalted butter
¾ cup yellow cornmeal
3 tablespoons chopped fresh chives
1 medium poblano, seeds removed, finely chopped (see tip, page 60)
  Kosher salt and freshly ground black pepper
3 eggs, separated
  Nonstick cooking spray

Preheat oven to 350° F. Remove husks from corn and place corn in a large pot with milk, cream, garlic, and thyme. Set over low heat and bring to a simmer. Shut off heat and cover to let corn steep for 10 to 15 minutes. Remove corn from milk mixture and cut the kernels off the cob with a sharp knife. Set corn aside.

Strain the milk mixture and set over high heat. Add butter, then pour in the cornmeal in a slow, steady stream, whisking at the same time. Cook and whisk constantly, until the cornmeal is blended in and the mixture is smooth and thick (it should look like porridge). Take the pot off the stove and fold in the reserved corn, chives, poblano, salt, and black pepper. Mix in the egg yolks, one at a time, so the corn mixture has the consistency of a batter. In a separate bowl beat the egg whites (use an electric mixer if you have one) until they hold stiff peaks. Fold the whites into the corn pudding to lighten it.

Coat the bottom and sides of an 8×8-inch baking dish with nonstick cooking spray. Spoon the batter into the prepared baking dish and bake in the preheated oven for 25 to 30 minutes. When it's done, the corn pudding will look puffy and golden brown like a soufflé. Serve with Prime Rib Chili (see page 60).

SPICY SWEET POTATO CHIPS | serves 4 • time: 25 minutes *(plus 30 minutes chilling time)*

4   large sweet potatoes
    Vegetable oil, for deep frying
    Chili Powder (see recipe, page 60), for seasoning
    Kosher salt and freshly ground black pepper

Take the unpeeled sweet potatoes and, using a vegetable peeler or
mandoline, make long, thin chips by slicing them lengthwise from top
to bottom. Place chips in a bowl of ice water and chill for 30 minutes.
Drain chips on a kitchen towel and pat dry.

Heat oil in a large pot over medium-high heat to 375°F. Fry chips
in single-layer batches for 2 to 3 minutes, until golden brown.
Remove chips with a slotted spoon; drain on paper towels. Season
with Chili Powder, salt, and pepper. Serve with Blue Cheese and
Chive Dip (see below).

BLUE CHEESE AND CHIVE DIP

1   cup sour cream
1   cup store-bought mayonnaise
1   cup crumbled blue cheese
1½ tablespoons honey
1   teaspoon lemon juice
½   bunch fresh chives (about 8 chives), finely chopped
    Kosher salt and freshly ground black pepper
    Finely chopped fresh chives, for garnish

Combine sour cream, mayonnaise, blue cheese, honey, lemon juice,
and the ½ bunch chives in a bowl and mix. Season with salt and
pepper. Garnish with chives. Serve with Spicy Sweet Potato Chips
(see above).

ONCE BOUGHT STOCK IN A COMPANY THAT CLAIMED TO HAVE FOUND THE CURE FOR THE COMMON COLD. WELL, IF YOU OR ANYONE IN YOUR FAMILY HAS HAD THE SNIFFLES THIS YEAR, YOU CAN PROBABLY GUESS THAT I LOST MY MONEY.

True story. We can walk on the moon and clone sheep, but for some reason we can't cure a runny nose. Well, the medical profession is not my calling, and I don't think I'm going to be the guy to rid us all of the sniffles, but what I can do is tell you about how I handle being under the weather.

Believe it or not, there really is an ongoing conversation in medical circles about whether chicken soup has medicinal qualities that actually help cure the common cold. Some studies have indicated that chicken soup contains an amino acid to inhibit the inflammation of cells in the nasal passage. So there you go. Maybe chicken soup does actually help. But regardless of what any medical journal tells me, I know what makes me feel better when I'm under the weather, and I think it might work for you too.

Once or twice a year, I'll get a cold that just zaps all of my energy, and it's all I can do just to get off the couch. Not too long ago I had one of those days, and I was home alone. We all know that misery loves company, but in this case I was out of luck. I'd watched Oprah, powered through a DVD marathon of *The Sopranos*, and called everyone I knew to tell them how awful I was feeling. Nothing was making it better. I soon realized that the only thing that was going to work was to get to the kitchen, get the blood flowing, and make myself some good, old-fashioned chicken soup.

OK, where do I go with this? Dumplings? Noodles? Kreplach? Matzo balls? So many choices, so little energy. Then it dawned on me—chicken tortellini, one of my favorite Italian pastas combined with the healing properties of chicken soup. But I can't stop there. I like where this is going. I'm well off the sick-food thing, and I'm in the zone. My mind is off of how bad I feel, and I'm hungry for the first time in days. Some baked goat cheese on a crostini will go beautifully with my soup, and I'll wrap it all up with a fresh and smooth strawberry-pound cake pudding. Vitamin C, right? Well, maybe not, but it sure tasted great.

I don't know if it was the soup or if the cold had simply run its course, but I woke up the next morning feeling like a million bucks. So I'm backing the soup theory, even if it's just so I have an excuse to make it again the next time I even think about a runny nose. Soup is good food—enjoy.

DR. TYLER'S CHICKEN MEATBALL AND TORTELLINI SOUP

serves 4 to 6 • time: 50 minutes

Chicken Meatballs
4 links organic chicken-apple sausage or equivalent ground chicken meat
½ cup fresh bread crumbs (2 slices fresh white bread ground up)
½ cup whole milk
1 egg
2 tablespoons chopped fresh Italian flat-leaf parsley
¼ cup grated Parmigiano-Reggiano, plus 2 tablespoons for sprinkling
Kosher salt and freshly ground black pepper
Extra-virgin olive oil

Soup
Extra-virgin olive oil
3 garlic cloves, peeled and smashed
4 fresh thyme sprigs
2 large carrots, cut into circles
1 medium onion, diced
2 ribs celery, diced
Kosher salt
2 quarts reduced-sodium chicken broth
4 black peppercorns
2 tablespoons chopped fresh Italian flat-leaf parsley
1 bay leaf
1 pound fresh refrigerated or frozen cheese tortellini, thawed
¼ cup finely chopped fresh Italian flat-leaf parsley
Grated Parmigiano-Reggiano
Fresh parsley sprigs, for garnish
1 crusty French baguette, to serve with the soup

> " I DON'T KNOW IF IT WAS THE SOUP OR IF THE COLD HAD SIMPLY RUN ITS COURSE, BUT I WOKE UP THE NEXT MORNING FEELING LIKE A MILLION BUCKS. "

Preheat oven to 375°F. Prepare meatballs by combining loose ground chicken meat (discard casings, if using sausages), bread crumbs, milk, egg, parsley, and the ¼ cup Parmigiano-Reggiano in a large mixing bowl. Season with salt and pepper, then mix until fully combined. Using a small ice cream scoop, make balls and set on a roasting tray. Drizzle lightly with oil and sprinkle with the 2 tablespoons Parmigiano-Reggiano. Roast in the preheated oven for 15 to 20 minutes, until golden brown and caramelized.

While the meatballs are roasting, prepare the soup. Set a large stockpot over medium heat. Add a 2-count of oil (about 2 tablespoons), the garlic, and thyme. Gently sauté until fragrant, about 2 minutes. Add carrot, onion, and celery. Season with salt and cook for 5 to 7 minutes. Pour in chicken broth and add peppercorns, the 2 tablespoons parsley, and bay leaf. Bring to a boil and then reduce heat and simmer for 25 minutes.

Once meatballs are cooked, scrape them into the pot of chicken soup and add tortellini. Bring to a boil and cook for 2 to 3 minutes to allow the flavors to come together. Remove peppercorns and bay leaf. Season with salt and pepper and serve in shallow bowls. Sprinkle with parsley and grated Parmigiano-Reggiano. Garnish each bowl with a parsley sprig and serve with some torn pieces of crusty bread.

I KNOW WHAT MAKES ME FEEL BETTER WHEN I'M UNDER THE WEATHER AND I THINK IT MIGHT WORK FOR YOU TOO

CHICKEN TORTELLINI NOODLE SOUP (RECIPE, P. 74/75)

BAKED GOAT CHEESE | serves 4 to 6 • time: 25 minutes

1 French baguette
   Extra-virgin olive oil
   Kosher salt and freshly ground black pepper
1 log or medallion (approximately 8 ounces) firm, good-quality
   goat cheese
1 cup store-bought olive tapenade

Preheat oven to 350°F. To make crostini, slice baguette into thin
rounds and set on a roasting tray. Drizzle with oil and season with
salt and pepper. Bake in the preheated oven for 7 to 8 minutes, until
golden brown, then set aside.

Place goat cheese on a roasting tray and top with freshly ground
black pepper. Bake for 5 to 7 minutes, until it is warmed through
and just starting to melt. Serve warm goat cheese with crostini and
olive tapenade.

> " BELIEVE IT OR NOT, THERE REALLY IS AN ONGOING
> CONVERSATION IN MEDICAL CIRCLES ABOUT WHETHER
> OR NOT CHICKEN SOUP HAS MEDICINAL QUALITIES THAT
> ACTUALLY HELP CURE THE COMMON COLD. "

STRAWBERRY-LEMON PUDDINGS

serves 4 • time: 35 minutes

2 cups strawberries, hulled and halved
1 Meyer lemon, juice only
2 tablespoons powdered sugar
1 pint heavy whipping cream
1 cup powdered sugar, plus 1 tablespoon for garnish
½ cup store-bought lemon curd
1 store-bought pound cake

Combine strawberries, lemon juice, and 2 tablespoons of powdered sugar in a small saucepan; place over medium heat. Cook and stir for 4 to 5 minutes, then remove from heat to cool. Remove 4 strawberry halves from saucepan and reserve for garnish.

Whip heavy cream in a large mixing bowl until soft peaks form. Fold in the 1 cup powdered sugar and the lemon curd, a little at a time, until combined. Set aside in the refrigerator while you prepare the cake.

Preheat oven to 350°F. Cut pound cake into ¼-inch-thick slices. Using an inverted 6-ounce ramekin, carefully cut out 8 rounds. (The rounds should fit snugly inside of the ramekin itself.) Break the remaining scraps of pound cake into coarse crumbs and toast on a baking sheet in the preheated oven about 5 minutes, until golden brown and fragrant.

To assemble, start with a layer of the lemon cream on the bottom of each of four 6-ounce ramekins, followed by a cake round, some strawberries, and lemon cream. Add another layer of cake. Drizzle the final cake layers with syrup from the strawberries and then top with a swirl of lemon cream and some toasted pound cake crumbs. Garnish each pudding with a reserved strawberry half and dust with powdered sugar.

6/
HAPPY HOUR

OKAY, LET'S MIX IT UP A BIT HERE. WE'RE GOING TO EAT DINNER EVERY DAY FOR THE REST OF OUR LIVES, MORE OR LESS, AND I THINK WE'VE BEEN DOING A PRETTY GOOD JOB GOING OVER SOME FANTASTIC NEW MENUS THAT YOU CAN PULL OUT FOR ANY NUMBER OF OCCASIONS.

But sometimes I don't want to worry about throwing any food together and I just want to have a few people over for some deep philosophical conversation and some appropriately sophisticated adult beverages. Yes, it's happy hour at my place, and it's going to be fun.

What a lot of people don't realize is that the cocktail is one of America's most important contributions to the world of food and drink. The history of the cocktail is, perhaps appropriately, a bit hazy. But what we do know is that the term was coined here in the United States around 1800. In fact, as early as 1806 an American magazine, *The Balance*, printed that a "cocktail is a stimulating liquor, composed of spirits of any kind, sugar, waters, and bitters." And in 1862 a San Francisco bartender by the name of "Professor" Jerry Thomas invented the Martinez, a gin concoction he made many times for a local gold miner on his way home to nearby Martinez. This, of course, would become the martini as we know it today and sparked the Golden Age of Cocktails, which ended with Prohibition in 1920. But by then cocktails were so popular that people weren't about to let a little thing like federal law keep them from their fun. Cocktails are not only legal today, but they are very much in fashion. Around the globe people are drinking cocktails of every shape, size, and flavor, ranging from the old-school Sazerac to the new-school Sex on the Beach. With our revived collective interest in cocktail culture, it has never been more fun to have a group of friends over to try some new flavors and combinations. There is still a distinction between what's technically a cocktail and what's not, but happy hour at my place is all about equal opportunity, and we're going to try all sorts of adult beverages. You can call 'em as you see 'em.

Just like when I'm cooking dinner, I'm always looking for new drink ideas to share with the guests in my home. Beer, wine, shots of whiskey—I've got it all. But to me, there's a brave new world out there worth exploring, and there's a lot of crossover to what I already do in the kitchen. Alcoholic drinks are all about balance, and much like baking, a little too much of this or that can send your entire recipe down the tubes. I like to look for new and interesting flavors and techniques and then work with them until I strike that perfect balance. And sometimes just putting my personal touch on a classic, like my Fresh Bloody Mary, is enough. Whichever way I go, it has to be delicious and not be so overwhelmingly alcoholic that I can't take more than one

sip. I think my Pickled Beet Martini is a great example of the intersection between kitchen and bar. I use pickled beets to create this deep, blood red martini that has a deliciously tangy flavor profile. It's not a cocktail your guests have likely had before, and I promise you they'll leave talking about it. And how about my White Russian Espresso? They may not have been using whipped cream siphons back in 1806, but in my mind, this is a cocktail for the new millennium.

 Whatever your drink of choice, be it neat, on the rocks, hot, or blended, there's always a spot for you at my happy hour. Like Jimmy Buffet says, "It's 5 o'clock somewhere."

WATERMELON NECTAR WITH LIME SALT | serves 2 to 4 • time: 8 minutes

Lime Salt
2 tablespoons sea salt
Zest of 1 lime

Drink
1 small seedless watermelon
4 ounces white tequila
2 ounces Simple Syrup (see below)
Splash of lime juice
1 lime, cut into wedges, for garnish

To prepare Lime Salt, using a mortar and pestle, combine salt and lime zest until the salt takes on a bright green color. Set aside.

To prepare watermelon nectar, cut up watermelon flesh and place in a strainer lined with a clean kitchen towel over a bowl. Gather the corners of the towel and squeeze tightly to extract watermelon nectar. Measure 8 ounces; reserve remaining nectar for another use. Combine watermelon nectar, tequila, Simple Syrup, and lime juice in a cocktail shaker. Shake and pour drink through a strainer over ice in glasses. Garnish with lime wedges and Lime Salt.

SIMPLE SYRUP Combine 1 part water and 1 part sugar in a saucepan. Bring to boiling over medium heat, stirring until sugar is dissolved (syrup is done when the mixture is clear and the surface is covered in bubbles). Remove from heat; cool in refrigerator until ready to use.

HOT TODDY | serves 4 • time: 15 minutes (photo on page 83)

4 slices red apple
3 cinnamon sticks
3 slices orange
2 cloves
16 ounces Simple Syrup (see above)
16 ounces bourbon whiskey

Combine all ingredients in a large saucepan and place over low heat. Slowly bring to a simmer to infuse the bourbon; keep over low heat for 5 to 7 minutes, until the mixture becomes fragrant. Serve warm.

WHITE RUSSIAN ESPRESSO | serves 4 • time: 5 minutes *(photo on page 89)*

4 ounces heavy whipping cream
8 ounces Kahlúa (coffee liqueur)
4 ounces vodka
4 espresso shots, in 4 separate cups
1 teaspoon roasted coffee beans, grated

Add cream, Kahlúa, and vodka to a pressurized whipped cream dispenser.* Shake the dispenser 3 to 4 times, then dispense on top of each hot espresso shot (it will come out like whipped cream). Top with grated coffee beans.

NOTE Find pressurized whipped cream dispensers at cooking stores.

PICKLED BEET MARTINI | serves 2 to 4 • time: 7 minutes

8 ounces pickled beet juice
6 ounces vermouth
6 ounces vodka
2 ounces aquavit
Pickled baby beets on a skewer, for garnish

Chill martini glasses by placing them in the freezer or putting ice cubes in the glasses. Combine beet juice, vermouth, vodka, and aquavit in a cocktail shaker with ice. Shake and pour drink through a strainer into glasses. Garnish with skewered baby beets.

POMEGRANATE SPRITZER | serves 4 • time: 2 minutes

1½ cups 100% pomegranate juice
1½ quarts San Pellegrino (seltzer water)
1 lime, cut into thin slices

Pour pomegranate juice into the bottom of a pitcher and top off with seltzer water. Add fresh slices of lime and serve in glasses over ice.

PICKLED BEET MARTINI, *LEFT* (RECIPE, P. 88)
POMEGRANATE SPRITZER, *ABOVE* (RECIPE, P. 88)
PINEAPPLE MOJITO, *BELOW* (RECIPE, P. 92)

PINEAPPLE MOJITO | serves 4 • time: 10 minutes

1 fresh pineapple
8 ounces white rum
1 cup ice cubes
4 ounces Simple Syrup (see page 87)
  Splash lime juice
3 fresh mint sprigs, leaves only

Using a sharp knife, remove the pineapple's tough outer skin and eyes.
Remove and discard core. Cut pineapple into cubes so they fit in a
blender. Put pineapple, rum, ice cubes, Simple Syrup, lime juice, and
mint in the blender. Process until you have a smooth puree.

CUCUMBER-LYCHEE SAKE | serves 4 • time: 12 minutes *(photo on page 93)*

4 long, thin slices fresh ginger
8 ounces Simple Syrup (see page 87)
2 English cucumbers
½ cup sake
¼ cup lychee juice
  Lychees, for garnish

Combine ginger and Simple Syrup in a small saucepan and place
over medium heat. Cook and stir until simmering. Remove from heat;
remove ginger from syrup. Set aside. Cut half of 1 cucumber into thin
slices; set aside. Peel the remaining 1½ cucumbers. Roughly chop
peeled cucumbers; puree in a blender.

Combine pureed cucumber, ginger-infused simple syrup, sake, and
lychee juice in a cocktail shaker. Shake and pour through a strainer
over ice into glasses. Garnish with cucumber slices and a couple
of lychees.

"Whatever your drink of choice, be it neat, on the rocks, hot, or blended, there's always a spot for you at my happy hour."

> GRAPE COCKTAIL (RIGHT)
> PEACH FIZZ (BELOW)

GRAPE COCKTAIL | serves 4 to 6 • time: 8 minutes

2 cups seedless red grapes, halved
2 tablespoons bar sugar
1 lemon, thinly sliced
8 ounces Cointreau
8 ounces Lillet Blanc
1 750-milliliter bottle white wine

Combine grape halves, sugar, and lemon slices in a large pitcher.
Using a wooden spoon, muddle (squash) the fruit to extract some of
the juice. Add Cointreau, Lillet Blanc, and top off with white wine. Stir
and serve over ice in glasses.

PEACH FIZZ | serves 4 to 6 • time: 7 minutes

1 cup frozen peach slices
1 teaspoon fruit pectin
2 tablespoons bar sugar
1 750-milliliter bottle Champagne, chilled

Combine frozen peaches, fruit pectin, and bar sugar in a blender.
Process until you have a smooth, frothy puree, about 1 minute. Place
mixture in a pressurized whipped cream dispenser* and shake as
directed. Dispense frothy puree in the bottom of each glass. Pour
Champagne over the top of the frothy puree (as the Champagne hits
the puree, it will bubble).

*NOTE Find pressurized whipped cream dispensers at cooking stores.

> " WHAT A LOT OF PEOPLE DON'T REALIZE IS THAT THE COCKTAIL
> IS ONE OF AMERICA'S MOST IMPORTANT CONTRIBUTIONS TO
> THE WORLD OF FOOD AND DRINK. "

ALCOHOLIC DRINKS ARE ALL ABOUT BALANCE, AND MUCH LIKE BAKING, A LITTLE TOO MUCH OF THIS OR THAT CAN SEND YOUR ENTIRE RECIPE DOWN THE TUBES.

> FRESH BLOODY MARY INGREDIENTS (RECIPE, P. 100)

> FRESH BLOODY MARY (RECIPE, P. 100)

FRESH BLOODY MARY | serves 4 to 6 • time: 10 minutes

Seasoned Salt Mix
1 teaspoon celery seeds, crushed
1 teaspoon sea salt
1 teaspoon coarsely ground black pepper
Splash lime juice

Fresh Bloody Mary
6 large heirloom tomatoes, cut into wedges
1 small English cucumber, roughly chopped
3 center ribs celery, roughly chopped
1 anchovy fillet, roughly chopped
1 1-inch piece fresh horseradish, peeled and minced
2 tablespoons fresh Italian flat-leaf parsley leaves
Dash hot sauce, or to taste
Dash Worcestershire sauce, or to taste
Kosher salt and freshly ground black pepper
1 lime, cut into wedges, for garnish
Center ribs celery, to serve with drinks

Prepare Seasoned Salt Mix by combining crushed celery seeds, salt, and pepper. Touch one point on the rim of each glass with lime juice and cover in Seasoned Salt Mix. Set aside.

For Fresh Bloody Mary, combine tomatoes, cucumber, celery, anchovy, horseradish, and parsley in a blender and puree completely. Season with hot sauce, Worcestershire sauce, salt, and pepper. Process once more to combine. Serve in glasses garnished with a lime wedge and a celery rib.

MOSCOW MULE | serves 4 • time: 5 minutes *(photo on page 101)*

3 bottles (12 ounces each) ginger beer
6 ounces lime juice
6 ounces vodka
2 fresh mint sprigs, leaves only
1 lime, cut into wedges, for garnish

Combine ginger beer, lime juice, and vodka in a large pitcher. Add mint leaves and pour over ice in glasses. Garnish with lime wedges.

7

A FUNNY THING HAPPENED ON THE WAY TO THE HOSPITAL …

MENU
> SMOKED RIBS WITH DRY RUB
> SPICY BLACK-EYED PEA RELISH
> HEIRLOOM TOMATO CHOW-CHOW
> SAVOY, LIME, AND CILANTRO COLESLAW
> BOURBON PEACH COBBLER

LIVE A PRETTY CRAZY LIFE. CRAZY SCHEDULE, CRAZY TRAVEL, CRAZY FRIENDS, CRAZY FUN.

So I'm pretty accustomed to dealing with anything and everything that comes my way. Maybe it's all those years in kitchens that have kept me on my toes. But every once in a while, something throws me for a loop. The unexpected happens, worlds collide, lightning strikes thrice, and everything seems to blow up in front of my eyes. May 21 of 2007 was one of those days.

It was a typical Florence family day. Well, wait. I take that back. We were sitting around the house, counting minutes between Tolan's contractions with both of our mothers. Stressful enough, right? Hayden was on his way and we were on high alert. So when the moms started screaming and yelling, I jumped into action, ready for the hospital. I had been waiting for some water to break, but I had no idea what I was in for. Outside of our house a guy had slammed his car right into a fire hydrant, and there were hundreds of thousands of gallons of water rushing onto our property. I dropped the overnight bag and raced out into the street to defend my property against the great flood. I'll admit, I got a bit fired up and threw my shoe at the guy who hit the hydrant. I know, not exactly an action hero move, but it was the best I could come up with on the fly. So water is pouring in, we're battening down the hatches, and there's a pregnant lady in the driveway yelling directions. Before I know it, sirens start screaming toward us—the Mill Valley Fire Department has arrived to save the day. Amidst the confusion of their arrival, I belatedly realize the firemen think Tolan is going into full-on labor and they're preparing to deliver our little boy right there in the flooded yard! Well, long story short, she finally convinced them she was not the emergency, and the guys refocused their attention on the water situation just in time to save our home. Hayden came into our world 12 hours later—cool, calm, and collected.

The boys down at the Mill Valley Fire Department saved my home and saved me from losing both of my shoes. To show my profound gratitude, I invited them all over for dinner at my place. Of course I had to give them something hearty—these guys work hard! But I also wanted to share a little piece of me with them, so a taste of the South made perfect sense. In South Carolina we typically do a sweet, mustard-based barbecue sauce, but after a recent trip to Graceland with my older son, Miles, I decided to mix it up with a Memphis-style dry rub. It's a nice change of pace, and this custom rub will blow you away. People think that a dry rub means dry ribs, but they're still deliciously moist and you'll be licking your fingers long after the ribs are gone. Smoky black-eyed peas make a great relish, and this chow-chow is something that really

wows everybody. It's essentially a Southern pickled tomato salad, but instead of using the traditional green tomatoes, I used some beautiful California heirlooms. The boys were on duty so we skipped the beers, but they got a taste of the good stuff in my Bourbon Peach Cobbler. Don't worry, the booze burns off in the oven!

I can't thank these guys enough for saving my house and being so protective of my wife and Hayden. If I could have them over every night, I would. If you ever have the time, I recommend you do something special for your local rescue crews too.

SMOKED RIBS WITH DRY RUB | serves 8 to 10 • time: 2 hours 45 minutes

Apple wood smoking chips, soaked in water

Dry Rub

- ¼ cup kosher salt
- 2 tablespoons freshly ground black pepper
- ¾ cup garlic powder
- ½ cup dried oregano
- ½ cup celery seeds
- 1 cup paprika
- 1 cup chile powder

Smoked Ribs

- ¼ cup water
- ¾ cup white distilled vinegar
- 2 lemons, juice only
- 4 slabs baby back pork ribs (about 8 pounds total)

Set up grill for indirect cooking over medium heat (no heat source under ribs). Place soaked apple wood chips in smoker box and place over heat on grill (if you are using a charcoal grill, place the wet chips directly on top of coals).

Combine Dry Rub ingredients. Set aside about one-third of the mixture for sprinkling on the ribs when finished. Add water, vinegar, and lemon juice to the remaining two-thirds of the rub to make a paste. Rub the paste on both sides of the ribs and set on the grill. Cook for 2½ hours, until ribs are tender. When the ribs are just about done, use a basting brush to give the ribs a final baste with the Dry Rub paste. Cook for 1 to 2 minutes more, turning once. Shower the ribs with the reserved Dry Rub, then serve immediately.

PEOPLE THINK THAT A DRY RUB MEANS DRY RIBS, BUT THEY ARE STILL MOIST AND YOU'LL BE LICKING YOUR FINGERS LONG AFTER THE RIBS ARE GONE.

SPICY BLACK-EYED PEA RELISH

serves 6 to 8 • time: 1 hour 20 minutes

3 cups dried black-eyed peas
2 slices thick-cut bacon
¼ bunch fresh thyme sprigs (4 sprigs)
2 tomatoes, quartered
5 garlic cloves, peeled
5 dried red chiles
Kosher salt and freshly ground black pepper
1 quart chicken broth
4 green onions, chopped
¼ cup chopped fresh cilantro
1 lemon, juice only
Extra-virgin olive oil
Cilantro sprigs, for garnish

Combine dried peas, bacon, thyme, tomatoes, garlic, and chiles in a large pot. Season with salt and black pepper and pour chicken broth over top. Place over medium-low heat and simmer for 1 hour, until peas are tender.

Drain cooked pea mixture, reserving the cooking liquid and discarding the thyme. Remove bacon slices, tomatoes, garlic, and chiles from the cooked peas; set aside. (Reserve chiles for garnish.) Cut up bacon slices and fold back into the peas with green onion, cilantro, and lemon juice. Place the cooking liquid, the tomatoes, and the garlic in a blender and puree. Dress the peas with the puree and give it a final season with salt and black pepper. Serve with a drizzle of oil. Garnish with reserved chiles and the cilantro sprigs.

HEIRLOOM TOMATO CHOW-CHOW | serves 4 to 6 • time: 45 minutes

1 quart apple cider vinegar
1 cup sugar
3 tablespoons celery seeds
3 tablespoons mustard seeds
1½ tablespoons pickling spice
1 tablespoon dry mustard
1 tablespoon ground turmeric
1 teaspoon salt
1 1-inch piece ginger, grated
2 pounds firm heirloom tomatoes (mixed colors and varieties), cut into large chunks
2 medium onions, sliced

Combine vinegar, sugar, celery seeds, mustard seeds, pickling spices, dry mustard, turmeric, salt, and ginger in a large pot. Place over high heat and bring to a boil. Reduce heat; simmer for 15 minutes to extract the flavors of the spices. Return heat to high and add tomatoes and onions, stirring to coat everything evenly. Once the liquid begins to boil, immediately shut off the heat and allow mixture to cool to room temperature.

SAVOY, LIME, AND CILANTRO COLESLAW | serves 4 to 6 • time: 12 minutes

1	head savoy cabbage
4	green onions
½	bunch fresh cilantro (8 sprigs)
½	cup sour cream
½	cup store-bought mayonnaise
1½	tablespoons sugar
2	limes
	Kosher salt and freshly ground black pepper

Shave cabbage with a sharp knife or mandoline so you have thin ribbons. Cut green onions long and on the bias so you have pieces similar in shape to the cabbage. Toss cabbage, green onion, and cilantro together in a large salad bowl. Set aside.

Make dressing by combining sour cream, mayonnaise, sugar, and the zest of the limes in a medium bowl. Season with salt and pepper and finish with a squeeze of lime juice. Pour dressing over cabbage mixture and toss to combine.

> **"THE BOYS DOWN AT THE MILL VALLEY FIRE DEPARTMENT SAVED MY HOME AND SAVED ME FROM LOSING BOTH OF MY SHOES. AND I CAN'T THINK OF ANY BETTER WAY TO SHOW MY GRATITUDE THAN BY HAVING THEM OVER FOR DINNER AT MY PLACE."**

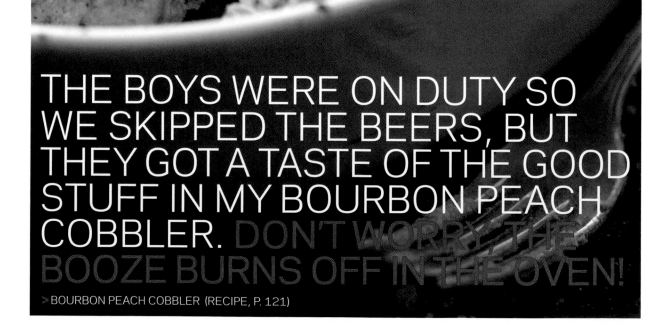

THE BOYS WERE ON DUTY SO WE SKIPPED THE BEERS, BUT THEY GOT A TASTE OF THE GOOD STUFF IN MY BOURBON PEACH COBBLER. DON'T WORRY, THE BOOZE BURNS OFF IN THE OVEN!

> BOURBON PEACH COBBLER (RECIPE, P. 121)

BOURBON PEACH COBBLER | serves 6 to 8 • time: 1 hour

8 peaches, peeled and sliced (6 to 8 cups)
¼ cup bourbon whiskey
¾ cup sugar, plus more for dusting
2 tablespoons cornstarch
1 teaspoon ground cinnamon, plus more for sprinkling
1½ cups all-purpose flour
2 teaspoons baking powder
½ teaspoon kosher salt
2 sticks (16 tablespoons) cold unsalted butter
¾ cup heavy whipping cream, plus more for brushing
1 quart vanilla bean ice cream

Preheat oven to 375°F. Combine peaches, bourbon, ¼ cup of the sugar, cornstarch, and cinnamon in a large bowl. Mix well to coat the peaches evenly.

Prepare the topping by sifting together the flour, the remaining ½ cup sugar, baking powder, and salt into a large bowl. Cut 1½ sticks (12 tablespoons) of the butter into small pieces. Add it to the flour mixture and cut it in with a pastry blender until the mixture looks like coarse bread crumbs. Pour in the cream and mix just until the dough comes together. Don't overwork; the dough should be slightly sticky but manageable.

Melt the remaining 4 tablespoons of butter in a 10-inch cast-iron skillet placed over medium-low heat. Add the peach mixture and cook gently until heated through, about 5 minutes. Transfer peach mixture to a 2-quart baking dish (or, if desired, leave mixture in cast-iron skillet). Drop the dough by tablespoonfuls over the warm peaches. (There can be gaps because the dough will puff up and spread out as it bakes.) Brush the top with a small amount of heavy cream and sprinkle with some sugar and a little extra cinnamon. Bake in the preheated oven on a tray (to catch any drips) for 40 to 45 minutes, until the top is brown and the fruit is bubbling. Serve warm with vanilla bean ice cream.

8

VEGETARIAN NIGHT:
THE CARNIVORE'S DILEMMA

MENU

> ARTICHOKE FRITTERS WITH MEYER LEMON SALT

> SUMMER SQUASH RISOTTO WITH CRISPY FRIED SAGE AND PARMESAN

> BEET CAKES WITH SWEET GREEK YOGURT

LOVE MEAT—RED MEAT, WHITE MEAT, DARK MEAT, THE OTHER WHITE MEAT, ALL OF IT. I LOVE TO COOK WITH IT AND EAT IT AND, TO BE HONEST, I DON'T SEE ANYTHING WRONG WITH THAT.

With that said, however, it's no secret that there are a lot of things about the various meat-producing industries that are a bit hard to swallow. I can understand why some people don't find meat to be all that attractive and have decided to become vegetarians. For some people, it's about compassion for animals. To others, it's about religious beliefs. Still others believe meat's bad for you. And there are those who just simply don't like the taste. It doesn't matter why people decide to become vegetarians. But it does matter that when they come to your house for dinner, you show them that you respect their choice and cook a vegetarian feast everyone will enjoy.

I've discovered that Northern California is a hotbed for vegetarians, and the issue probably comes up more at my dinner table than in many parts of the country. So when planning a dinner party, I always make sure to ask my guests beforehand if they have any dietary restrictions. If they don't eat meat, I welcome the challenge to work out a vegetarian menu that is both satisfying and delicious. I can't bear the thought of forcing veggie-eating guests to subsist on a desperate meal of side dishes and hoarded scraps from the bread basket. And I'm also not about to alienate them and make them their own "special" meal. We're all eating together and we're going to share the same great food.

Some meat eaters are intent on believing that vegetarian dishes are severely lacking in vital nutrients. Well, for the record, that is just not true. There are plenty of nutrients to go around, so don't worry, you won't become instantly frail and listless because you didn't eat a side of red meat for dinner. Truth be told, a well-balanced vegetarian diet can give you all of the nutrients you need. Some studies have even shown that you may live longer and lower your risk of certain diseases by subsisting on a meatless diet.

Nutrients aside, there are a lot of beautiful flavors in vegetables, fruits, nuts, and grains, and I can't find one good reason why you should be scared to try to make an entire meal out of them. Meat is great, but you'll do just fine without it. Start with my crispy fried artichoke fritters—hot, savory, and bursting with flavor when accented with an out-of-this-world Meyer lemon salt. Follow the fritters up with a rich, creamy Summer Squash Risotto that's satisfying to the last bite. And for the grand finale, the Beet Cakes with Sweet Greek Yogurt will wow everybody.

So the next time somebody says the "V" word, embrace it and make the best of it. I promise you might even like it.

ARTICHOKE FRITTERS
WITH MEYER LEMON SALT | serves 4 to 6 • time: 45 minutes

Vegetable oil, for deep frying

Meyer Lemon Salt
3   Meyer lemons, zest only
3   tablespoons sea salt

Fritters
¾   cup all-purpose flour
¼   cup cornstarch
2   tablespoons baking powder
2   teaspoons kosher salt
2   egg yolks
1   cup soda water
2   globe artichokes
    Lemon juice
2   fresh mint sprigs, for garnish
    Malt vinegar, to serve with fritters

Heat a large pot of vegetable oil over medium heat to 350°F.

To prepare the Meyer Lemon Salt, using a mortar and pestle, combine lemon zest and salt. Mix together until the salt and lemon become a bright yellow.

For fritters, make the batter by combining flour, cornstarch, baking powder, and salt in a large mixing bowl. Make a well in the center and add the yolks. Slowly pour in the soda water as you whisk, gradually incorporating the flour from around the edges of the bowl to make a smooth batter.

Trim down artichokes by removing the outer leaves and cutting off the tough lower part of the stem so you just have the hearts. Use a sharp knife or mandoline to cut hearts into thin slices from the top of the flower through the stem so you have heart shapes. (As you work with the artichoke hearts, rub the exposed sides with lemon juice to prevent them from turning brown.) Dip in batter, shaking off excess, and fry in hot oil for 3 to 4 minutes, until fritters are golden brown and puffy. Drain on paper towels, season with Meyer Lemon Salt, and garnish with mint. Serve with malt vinegar.

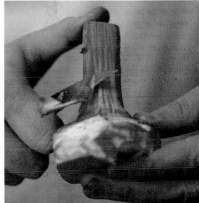
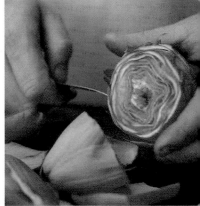

ARTICHOKE FRITTERS, *ABOVE AND BELOW LEFT* (RECIPE, P. 126)
MEYER LEMON SALT, *BELOW RIGHT* (RECIPE, P. 126)
SUMMER SQUASH RISOTTO WITH CRISPY SAGE AND PARMESAN, *OPPOSITE* (RECIPE, P. 131)

SUMMER SQUASH RISOTTO WITH
CRISPY FRIED SAGE AND PARMESAN

serves 4 to 6 • time: 50 minutes

4 summer squash
1 zucchini
6 pattypan squash
1 large onion, sliced
¼ bunch fresh thyme sprigs (4 sprigs), leaves only
   Extra-virgin olive oil
   Kosher salt and freshly ground black pepper

   Risotto
   Extra-virgin olive oil
1 bunch fresh sage sprigs, leaves only
1 medium onion
2 cups Arborio rice
½ 750-milliliter bottle dry white wine
2 quarts reduced-sodium vegetable broth
½ stick unsalted butter, cut into thirds
1 cup grated Parmigiano-Reggiano cheese
   Kosher salt and freshly ground black pepper

Preheat oven to 350°F. Cut squash, zucchini, and pattypan squash into circles and slice onion. Set out on a roasting tray and scatter thyme leaves over the top. Drizzle with olive oil and season with salt and pepper. Roast in the preheated oven for 15 to 20 minutes, until golden brown and fragrant.

While the vegetables roast, start the risotto. Set a large, heavy-based pot over medium heat. Pour a 3-count of oil (about 3 tablespoons) into the pot and fry the sage leaves until they are crispy and crackly. Drain leaves on paper towels and set aside. Add onion to the pot and sauté until fragrant and slightly translucent. Add rice and cook for 2 to 3 minutes over medium heat as you stir with a wooden spoon. Add the wine; cook until mostly evaporated. Begin adding vegetable broth, a little at a time, allowing the rice to absorb the broth each time before adding more. Continue to do this until the rice is tender but still has a little bite. (Add water, if necessary, if you use all the vegetable broth before the rice is done.) To finish, add butter and Parmigiano-

"Nutrients aside, there are a lot of beautiful flavors in vegetables, fruits, nuts, and grains ..."

BEET CAKES WITH SWEET GREEK YOGURT | serves 4 • time: 50 minutes

1 recipe Beet Garnish (takes 2 hours to make) (see recipe, below)

Cakes
2 tablespoons unsalted butter, to grease baking pans
1¼ cups all-purpose flour
½ teaspoon baking powder
⅓ teaspoon baking soda
Kosher salt
¼ teaspoon ground allspice
¼ teaspoon ground cinnamon
¼ teaspoon ground nutmeg
2 tablespoons pomegranate molasses or regular molasses
2 large eggs
½ cup buttermilk
⅓ cup vegetable oil
¾ cup packed dark brown sugar
1¼ cups finely chopped, peeled red beets

Sweet Greek Yogurt
2 cups unsweetened Greek yogurt
¼ cup honey
1 teaspoon vanilla extract

Prepare Beet Garnish ahead of time; remove from oven and set aside. Preheat oven to 350°F. Lightly grease four 8-ounce individual baking dishes with butter (ovenproof ramekins or cocotte dishes work well). Combine flour, baking powder, baking soda, salt, and spices in a large mixing bowl. Mix molasses, eggs, buttermilk, oil, and brown sugar together in a separate bowl. Add buttermilk mixture to flour mixture; whisk to combine. Fold in the beets.

Set baking dishes on a roasting tray. Divide batter among dishes and bake in the preheated oven for 20 to 25 minutes, until the cakes are puffed and a cake tester inserted in centers comes out clean.

Make Sweet Greek Yogurt by combining yogurt, honey, and vanilla in a bowl. Swirl with a wooden spoon so ingredients are just combined. Serve yogurt with warm cakes. Top each cake with Beet Garnish.

BEET GARNISH Preheat oven to 150°F. Shave 1 small beet into thin slices using a mandoline or sharp knife. Line a roasting tray with parchment paper and set the beet slices out in a single layer on the pan. Cover with another sheet of parchment paper, carefully pressing out any air bubbles. Top with another tray to add weight. Bake in the preheated oven for 2 to 3 hours to dehydrate the beet slices without overcooking them.

THE BIGGEST OBSTACLE TO
MAKING A GREAT VEGETARIAN
MEAL IS IN YOUR HEAD.

9

PREGNANCY PASTA

MENU

> GARDEN PUREE BRUSCHETTA
> PANCETTA CARBONARA WITH FRESH BABY
SPINACH (aka "MY WIFE'S PREGNANCY PASTA")
> PANNA COTTA WITH FRESH STRAWBERRIES
AND BALSAMIC SYRUP

T

HE DOCTORS ARE LYING WHEN THEY TELL YOU THAT PREGNANCY LASTS NINE MONTHS. IT'S REALLY A 10-MONTH PROCESS, SOUP TO NUTS, AND I'LL TELL YOU, THAT'S 10 MONTHS OF CRAVINGS AND LATE-NIGHT KITCHEN MISSIONS.

Between Hayden and our new baby, Dorothy, my wife has been pregnant the majority of our married life thus far, and despite where you might think I'm going here, it has been really special cooking for her and our unborn children. She's handled it all gracefully, and we couldn't be happier building our little family. But when a craving hits, you never know what the request is going to be. As a cook and a dad, I have to be on my toes. It's usually something very specific, and it needs to come out on the double. There's no time for shopping, and I'm handicapped by the long list of foods that can harm a pregnant mom-to-be and her baby, so I'm racing the clock to create the perfect dish. It's like *Food 911* meets *Iron Chef*, and the chairman is my pregnant wife.

When Tolan was pregnant with Hayden, she had a craving for spaghetti carbonara. Great, a no-brainer, I thought to myself, and I got to work in the kitchen. This is one of my favorite Italian dishes, and I always make sure to keep my kitchen stocked with the basic ingredients for it. Eggs, a block of fresh Parmesan cheese, pork fat—it's all in the house. But just as the water starts to boil, I'm reminded that pregnant women can't eat raw eggs because they can pass along bacteria to an unborn child. Since a big part of a carbonara is tossing raw yolk into the hot pasta, I'll have to improvise. I know this is going to make a lot of Italian grandmothers gasp, but I've got to do what I've got to do. So to make this dish baby-safe, I add the extra step of whisking the egg in the top of a double boiler first just to make sure it's totally safe. Oops—I'm out of peas as well, but not a problem; a little bit of baby spinach will do just fine. It actually adds a nice twist to the dish that I think you'll like. Mission accomplished. To round out the meal, I throw in a little springtime with gorgeous green Garden Puree Bruschetta and light and sweet strawberry-balsamic panna cotta. There you go. Everything to make Mommy happy and keep Baby healthy and kicking.

I'm sorry about taking liberties with the classic carbonara, but you know what? I think Tolan and I have created a new classic. At least I know it's an instant classic in our household, and I hope it will be in yours too.

GARDEN PUREE BRUSCHETTA | serves 4 to 6 • time: 45 minutes

½ pound sugar snap peas, trimmed
1 pound English peas, shelled, or 1 cup frozen petite peas
½ pound asparagus, tips only (2¼-inch-long pieces)
½ pound haricots verts or tender green beans, trimmed
⅔ cup whole-milk ricotta cheese
3 green onions, green parts only, roughly chopped
   Extra-virgin olive oil
   Kosher salt and freshly ground black pepper
½ bunch chopped fresh chives (about 8 chives), for garnish

Crostini
1 French baguette
   Extra-virgin olive oil
2 garlic cloves

Place a large pot of salted water over high heat and bring to a boil. Add the sugar snap peas, English peas (if using), asparagus tips, and haricots verts and cook about 3 minutes, until bright green and crisp-tender. (If you're using frozen peas, add them during the last minute of cooking.) Drain, transfer to a bowl of salted ice water to stop cooking, and drain again. Puree vegetables in a food processor with the ricotta, green onion, a drizzle of oil, salt, and pepper to taste. Garnish with chives.

Prepare the Crostini by cutting the baguette into thin slices. Drizzle slices with oil and place on a roasting tray. Bake in the preheated oven until golden brown on both sides. Remove from oven and rub with a peeled, cut clove of garlic while bread is still warm. Serve crostini with vegetable and cheese puree.

> **WHEN A CRAVING HITS, YOU NEVER KNOW WHAT THE REQUEST IS GOING TO BE. SO AS A COOK AND A DAD, I'VE GOT TO BE ON MY TOES. IT'S USUALLY SOMETHING VERY SPECIFIC, AND IT NEEDS TO COME OUT ON THE DOUBLE.**

PANCETTA CARBONARA WITH FRESH BABY SPINACH (aka "MY WIFE'S PREGNANCY PASTA") (RECIPE, P. 146)

PANCETTA CARBONARA WITH FRESH BABY SPINACH (aka "MY WIFE'S PREGNANCY PASTA")

serves 4 • time: 1 hour 15 minutes

1 recipe Fresh Pasta Dough (see recipe, page 27),
rolled out to thinnest setting as directed
All-purpose flour
Extra-virgin olive oil
⅓ pound pancetta, cut into thin strips
7 garlic cloves, thinly sliced

Parmesan Sabayon
6 large eggs
1 cup milk
1 cup heavy whipping cream
½ cup grated Parmesan
Freshly ground black pepper

3 cups baby spinach
Extra-virgin olive oil
Freshly ground black pepper
¼ cup grated Parmesan

Prepare Fresh Pasta Dough, cutting the pasta sheets into spaghetti. Toss spaghetti in a little flour to prevent the noodles from sticking together and spread pasta on a baking sheet to dry while preparing the sauce.

Set a large pan over medium heat, add a 1-count of oil (about 1 tablespoon), and fry the pancetta, stirring occasionally, until crispy. About halfway through add the garlic and cook until golden. Drain pancetta and garlic on a paper towel; set aside. Place a large pot of salted water over high heat and bring to a boil. Drop the pasta into the boiling water and cook until tender, yet firm (al dente), 2 to 3 minutes for fresh pasta. Drain; place pasta in a bowl.

While the pasta is cooking, make the Parmesan Sabayon. Create a double boiler with a medium saucepan and a large bowl (bowl should rest in saucepan and the bottom of the bowl should not touch the water). Bring about 1 inch water to a simmer in the medium saucepan. Combine eggs, milk, and cream in the bowl. Set bowl over saucepan and vigorously mix with an immersion blender for 7 to 8 minutes, until it just starts to thicken. (It should be frothy, thick, and creamy when done.) Add the ½ cup Parmesan and pepper and mix once more to combine. Pour the sabayon over the noodles and mix gently with tongs so the pasta is coated in the sauce. Portion pasta among bowls. Top with a spoonful of crispy pancetta and garlic and a small handful of baby spinach. Finish with a drizzle of oil, a few turns of freshly ground pepper, and grated Parmesan.

PANNA COTTA WITH FRESH
STRAWBERRIES AND BALSAMIC SYRUP

serves 4 • time: 25 minutes *(plus 8 hours refrigeration time)*

1 cup whole milk
1 cup heavy whipping cream
½ cup superfine sugar
1 vanilla bean
3 strips lemon peel
¼ cup lemon juice
1¼ teaspoons powdered gelatin
  Nonstick cooking spray, for greasing ramekins
1 cup crème fraîche, room temperature
1 cup sliced strawberries
2 tablespoons high-quality balsamic vinegar*

Put the milk, cream, and sugar in a pot; set over medium heat. Split and scrape the vanilla bean seeds into the pot and add lemon peel. Bring to a simmer, then shut off heat and cover with a lid. Set aside to steep for 15 to 20 minutes.

While the mixture is steeping, combine the lemon juice and gelatin in a bowl, whisking constantly to avoid lumps. Take four 6-ounce ramekins and spray with nonstick spray to evenly coat the insides.

Put the crème fraîche in a large mixing bowl. Pass the cooled cream mixture through a sieve into the bowl and discard the vanilla bean and lemon peel in the sieve. Gently whisk to combine the mixture. Distribute evenly among ramekins, cover with plastic wrap, and refrigerate for 8 hours or overnight, until they are set.

When set, arrange sliced strawberries on top of each serving and drizzle with balsamic vinegar.

*NOTE If the balsamic vinegar is not high quality, try simmering it over low heat to reduce it until it is syrupy and fuller in flavor.

> 66 **THERE YOU GO. EVERYTHING TO MAKE MOMMY HAPPY AND KEEP BABY HEALTHY AND KICKING.** 99

10

ROCK 'N' ROLL TACO

EVERY SUMMER I TRY TO LIGHTEN UP MY SCHEDULE AND TAKE A LONG, RELAXING TRIP THAT LETS ME PUT MY FEET UP AND JUST LIVE THE DREAM.

A couple of summers ago, my son Miles and I decided that Mexico would be a great place for us to hang out with our friends, get some sun, surf, and maybe even get a little tan. We brought a big crew with us and rented a huge villa on the beach, where we cooked, swam, and wasted away the days. The food was delicious and the margaritas (and soda for Miles) were plentiful. That trip will go down in our father-and-son hall of fame. Sometimes when I've been burning the candle at both ends, I think back to that trip and just want to recapture a bit of it at home—and the easiest way to do that is through food. There's just something festive and fun about Mexican food that makes people happy. So when I feel the need to take myself to another time and place, Mexico is one of my first stops, and I try to bring everyone with me.

The Mexican people live by the taco, and accordingly they've taken it in a million different directions. Frankly I've seldom had a bad one south of the border. From a quick breakfast taco of eggs and potatoes to a late-night plate of *tacos al pastor*, the possibilities are endless, and they work any time of day as a snack or full meal. Mexican tacos vary from region to region, but no matter where you find them, they'll always be some form of filling wrapped in a corn or flour tortilla. Here in the States, slap anything between two slices of bread and it's a sandwich. Well, the Mexicans apply that same principle to their tacos.

For this menu, I'm using traditional corn tortillas and taking a home-style approach with slow-cooked pot roast that falls apart and melts in your mouth. The moist shredded beef is warm, satisfying, and has just the right amount of heat. Although many Mexican tacos consist of just the filling and tortillas alone, I like to top off my tacos with a little bit of queso fresco and guacamole to build the perfect package of flavors and textures. Hey, it's my house, and I can do whatever I want! Some sliced radishes and carrots for garnish and a spicy chile relleno round out my plate, and I'm on my way to a long siesta.

But wait, this is a party! Although I love a few Mexican beers, it's a cold, refreshing margarita that I know will really put everyone in a good mood. There's a lot of debate over the origin of the margarita, so I'll spare you the inconclusive history lesson. But since about the late 1930s, it

has become the signature cocktail of Mexico's most celebrated export, tequila, and has become the most ordered cocktail in America. Again I'll spare you the history lesson on tequila, but it is pretty darn interesting, so I recommend reading up on the blue agave plant used to make the famous alcohol. You might be surprised to learn that tequila isn't just that harsh, college party poison you remember. In fact, it's a smooth and sophisticated liquor. My buddy Sammy Hagar makes some of the world's best tequila, so I figured there's nobody better to hit up for a tutorial on Cabo Wabo margarita making. Rock 'n' roll, Sammy!

MEXICAN POT ROAST TACOS | serves 6 to 8 • time: 2 hours 30 minutes

Pot Roast
Extra-virgin olive oil
3 pounds shoulder of beef
Kosher salt and freshly ground black pepper
1 large onion, cut into wedges
2 cloves garlic, smashed
1 28-ounce can whole San Marzano tomatoes
3 dried red chiles
1 tablespoon ground cumin
1 tablespoon ancho chile powder
⅓ bunch fresh cilantro (about 8 sprigs)
Water
2 tablespoons red wine vinegar

For serving
8 fresh medium corn tortillas
3 cups finely shredded romaine lettuce
½ bunch fresh cilantro
⅓ pound Cotija cheese, crumbled
2 limes, cut into wedges for garnish

Drizzle beef shoulder with oil, then season with plenty of salt and black pepper. Set a large, heavy-based pot over medium-high heat. Sear on all sides until you have a nice brown crust, adding additional oil to the pan as necessary to prevent sticking. Add onion and garlic to the pot and stir until they caramelize a little and have contact with the bottom of the pot. Add tomatoes with juice, chiles, cumin, chile powder, and the ½ bunch cilantro. Add 2 inches of water to the pot. Crush tomatoes with the back of a wooden spoon. Cover and simmer about 2 hours, until the meat is fork-tender and comes apart with little resistance. Once cooked, use a wooden spoon to break apart the meat. Season with salt and black pepper to taste; add the vinegar.

If you like, warm the tortillas over an open flame on a gas stove, about 10 seconds per side. Serve the meat in tortillas with romaine, cilantro, cheese, and lime wedges.

SAN MARZANO "QUICK" SALSA | serves 4 to 6 • time: 7 minutes

1 28-ounce can whole San Marzano tomatoes, drained with liquid reserved
1 small red onion, roughly chopped
½ serrano chile, or to taste (see tip, page 60)
2 limes, juice only
¼ bunch fresh cilantro (about 4 sprigs)
¼ cup extra-virgin olive oil
   Kosher salt and freshly ground black pepper
   Fresh cilantro, for garnish
1 lime wedge, for garnish

Combine drained tomatoes, onion, chile, lime juice, the ¼ bunch cilantro, and oil in a food processor and pulse until well combined. Season with plenty of salt and black pepper. Use reserved tomato liquid to adjust consistency as desired. Garnish with cilantro and lime wedge. Serve with Fresh Fried Corn Chips (see recipe, page 165).

" But wait, this is a party! Although I love a few Mexican beers, it's a cold, refreshing margarita that I know will really put everyone in a good mood. **"**

THE ULTIMATE GUACAMOLE | serves 4 to 6 • time: 10 minutes *(plus 1 hour refrigeration time)*

6   ripe avocados
3   limes, juice only
1   medium onion, chopped
1   garlic clove, minced
2   serrano chiles, thinly sliced (see tip, page 60)
¼   bunch fresh cilantro (about 4 sprigs), finely chopped
¼   cup extra-virgin olive oil
    Kosher salt and freshly ground black pepper

Halve and pit the avocados using a knife. With a tablespoon, scoop the flesh into a large bowl. Add lime juice, onion, garlic, chiles, cilantro, and oil to the bowl. Season with salt and black pepper. Use a potato masher to break up the avocados and mix everything together. Continue until just combined so you still have plenty of texture. Give it a taste and season once more with salt and black pepper, if necessary.

Lay a piece of plastic wrap over the bowl and press onto the surface of the guacamole, squeezing out air bubbles (this prevents the guacamole from turning brown). Before serving, refrigerate about 1 hour to allow the flavors to come together. Serve with Fresh Fried Corn Chips (see below).

FRESH FRIED CORN CHIPS | serves 4 to 6 • time: 35 minutes

    Vegetable oil, for deep frying
12 corn tortillas
    Kosher salt

Heat oil in a large pot to 375°F. Cut corn tortillas into large wedges. Fry wedges in batches for 2 to 3 minutes, until golden and crispy. Remove chips with a slotted spoon; drain on paper towels. Season chips with salt as soon as they come out of the fryer. Serve chips warm with The Ultimate Guacamole (above) and San Marzano "Quick" Salsa (see recipe, page 160).

IT'S PRETTY SAFE TO SAY THAT
MOST PEOPLE LOVE MEXICAN FOOD.
THERE'S JUST SOMETHING FESTIVE
AND FUN ABOUT IT THAT MAKES
PEOPLE HAPPY.

CHILES RELLENOS | serves 4 to 6 • time: 40 minutes

6 poblanos
2 pounds queso fresco, room temperature
  Kosher salt
6 egg whites
1 cup all-purpose flour
  Extra-virgin olive oil

For serving
¼ small onion
3 baby radishes
2 tablespoons crumbled queso fresco
2 tablespoons fresh cilantro leaves

Preheat oven to 375°F. Set the poblanos over an open gas flame on your stovetop for 30 to 45 seconds per side, rotating with metal tongs until they are blistered all over (or place poblanos on a roasting tray under the broiler for 4 to 5 minutes and turn occasionally until blistered on all sides). Once blistered, place hot poblanos in a bowl and cover tightly with plastic wrap to let the poblanos steam, about 2 minutes. Use a kitchen towel to "rub" off the blistered skin, then use a sharp paring knife to make a slit the length of each poblano. Remove the ribs and seeds carefully so you don't tear the poblanos. Sprinkle poblanos lightly with salt. Stuff the inside of each poblano with queso fresco. Secure the openings with toothpicks.

Set a large skillet over medium-high heat and cover the bottom of the pan with ¼ inch oil. Meanwhile, whisk egg whites in a large bowl until stiff peaks form. Place the flour in a medium bowl. Dredge the stuffed poblanos in flour, coat in egg whites, and fry in the hot oil for 3 to 4 minutes on each side, until golden on both sides. Bake in the preheated oven for 10 minutes, until heated through.

Using a mandoline or sharp knife, shave onion and radishes into rings. Garnish poblanos with onion, radishes, queso fresco, and cilantro. Serve with Roasted Tomatillo Salsa (see recipe, page 172).

> " ... A SPICY CHILE RELLENO TO ROUND OUT MY PLATE, AND I'M ON MY WAY TO A LONG SIESTA. "

CHILES RELLENOS
(RECIPE, P. 168)

ROASTED TOMATILLO SALSA

serves 6 to 8 • time: 35 minutes

1 pound tomatillos, husked and rinsed
1 jalapeño, split down the middle (see tip, page 60)
1 small Spanish onion, sliced
4 garlic cloves
  Extra-virgin olive oil
½ tablespoon kosher salt
½ bunch fresh cilantro
2 limes, juice only
¼ cup extra-virgin olive oil

Preheat oven to 375°F. On a roasting tray, arrange tomatillos, jalapeño, onion, and garlic. Drizzle with a 3-count of oil (about 3 tablespoons) and season with salt. Roast for 10 to 12 minutes, until tomatillos are tender and slightly blistered.

Put the cooked vegetables in a blender with the cilantro and lime juice. Pour in oil and process until you have a smooth puree (be careful when you process the hot vegetables in the blender; hold down the lid with a kitchen towel over the top). Taste and, if desired, adjust seasoning with extra lime juice or salt according to preference. Serve with Chiles Rellenos (see recipe, page 168).

> " Here in the States, slap anything between two slices of bread and it's a sandwich. Well, the Mexicans apply that same principle to their tacos. "

SAMMMY HAGAR'S CABO WABO MARGARITA | serves 1 • time: 2 minutes

2 ounces Cabo Wabo Reposado Tequila
2 ounces triple sec
1 ounce freshly squeezed lime juice
1 lime wedge
  Salt
  Splash blue curaçao
1 lime slice, for garnish

Pour tequila, triple sec, and lime juice to a cocktail shaker; fill shaker with ice and shake. Using a lime wedge, rub a little lime juice in one spot on the rim of the glass and dip in salt so the glass has a "kiss" of salt. Strain margarita into the glass and finish with a splash of blue curaçao. Garnish with lime slice.

11 / WORKIN' LATE

MENU

> PENNE WITH SPICY ITALIAN SAUSAGE, CREAM, TOMATOES, AND PEAS
> BIBB LETTUCE WITH TARRAGON VINAIGRETTE
> SWEET LEMON RICOTTA WITH MIXED BERRIES AND BISCOTTI

IN AMERICA, WE WORK ABOUT 25% MORE HOURS THAN THE EUROPEANS, AND, IN TURN WE MAKE MORE MONEY.

But the catch is, we spend all of that extra dough compensating for the things we don't have time to do. We spend more money dining out, ordering takeout, hiring housekeepers, and arranging child care because we don't have the time to cook, clean, or care for our own children. It's a sad, vicious cycle, I know. I'm not going to tell you I have the solution, but I'll do my best to get you to a place where you can at least feel confident that you can get dinner on your table after a long day.

I work hard, just like you, and I'm really happy to be doing what I do. But it is still, indeed, work, and between shooting shows, writing books, making appearances, and flying from one end of the globe to another, I'm as pressed for time as you are. At the end of a long day, I face the same challenges when it comes to getting dinner on the table. But I've thought this through. I take extra steps every day to get myself and my kitchen ready to rock at a moment's notice.

The first step is to create a system in which you know what staples you have in stock at all times, from bags of pasta to cans of San Marzano tomatoes to cream to frozen peas. Staples like these work in any number of dishes, and they can serve as building blocks of flavor for your meals. If you have confidence in your stocked kitchen, those last few bursts of energy you have for grocery shopping at the end of the day will be put to good use. You'll know that if you pick up some fresh X, you can put it with a box of Y, pull out the frozen Z, and boom, dinner is ready in just a few minutes.

Cooking doesn't need to be a long, drawn-out process, and you shouldn't have to eat up your entire evening slaving away in the kitchen. I love this menu because it tastes like you toiled away in the kitchen for hours, but in reality it's relatively quick and painless. As quickly as you can boil some water for pasta, you can put this menu together by picking up a few fresh ingredients at the market and building the rest of the meal around them. The fresh sausage is savory and delicious and really takes a pot of pasta to the next level. Cream (stocked in the fridge), peas (always on hand in the freezer), and some sweet San Marzanos (a permanent pantry fixture) and you have your main dish. Fresh Bibb lettuce and a quick vinaigrette all from stocked staples. Perfect. And even dessert is quick and easy.

This menu is just one example of how no matter how late you work, you can get something fresh and delicious on your table. Plan ahead to let your kitchen and the market work for you, and use your building blocks of flavor to create a meal that's quick, easy, and satisfying. You've worked hard all day, and it's time you got a break.

PENNE WITH SPICY ITALIAN
SAUSAGE, CREAM, TOMATOES, AND PEAS

serves 4 to 6 • time: 55 minutes

- 4 links spicy Italian sausage
- 1 pound dried penne
  Extra-virgin olive oil
- 1 medium onion, chopped
- 4 garlic cloves, peeled and chopped
- 1 28-ounce can crushed San Marzano tomatoes
- ¼ cup torn fresh basil leaves
  Kosher salt and freshly ground black pepper
- 1 cup heavy whipping cream
- 2 cups peas, blanched*
- ½ cup grated Parmigiano-Reggiano, plus more for serving
  Fresh basil leaves, for garnish

Preheat oven to 350°F. Place the sausages in a roasting pan and roast in the preheated oven for 12 to 15 minutes, until slightly golden and just cooked. Cut sausage at an angle into bite-size pieces.

Place a large pot of salted water over high heat and bring to a boil. Drop the pasta into the boiling water and cook until tender yet firm (al dente).

Set a large, heavy-based pot over medium heat and add a 2-count of olive oil (about 2 tablespoons). Add onion and garlic and sauté until translucent and fragrant. Add tomatoes and basil; season with salt and pepper. Simmer for 15 minutes, then fold in cream and continue to simmer until rich and creamy. Add sausage, blanched peas, and Parmigiano-Reggiano. Fold together and cook for 2 to 3 minutes to allow the flavors to come together. Serve topped with a shower of cheese and garnish with basil.

*TIP To blanch the peas, submerge them into boiling water for 2 ½ minutes (1 minute for frozen peas), then strain them and plunge them into ice water to stop the cooking process. Strain them again and set aside.

BIBB LETTUCE WITH TARRAGON VINAIGRETTE | serves 4 to 6 • time: 15 minutes

1 small shallot, peeled and diced
1 teaspoon Dijon mustard
1 lemon, juice only
¼ cup extra virgin olive oil
2 tablespoons honey
1 tablespoon chopped fresh tarragon
Kosher salt and freshly ground black pepper
1 head Bibb lettuce
1 tablespoon fresh tarragon leaves

Combine shallot, mustard, and lemon juice in a large salad bowl. Slowly drizzle in oil as you constantly whisk to emulsify the dressing. Once all the oil has been incorporated, stir in honey and fold in the 1 tablespoon chopped tarragon. Season with salt and pepper.

Wash the lettuce and separate the leaves. Smear the dressing up around the insides of the salad bowl and toss the leaves in the bowl. (By doing this the leaves pick up a light, even coating of the dressing.) Fold in the 1 tablespoon tarragon leaves and serve.

> " COOKING DOESN'T NEED TO BE A LONG, DRAWN-OUT PROCESS, AND YOU SHOULDN'T HAVE TO EAT UP YOUR ENTIRE EVENING SLAVING AWAY IN THE KITCHEN. "

SWEET LEMON RICOTTA
WITH MIXED BERRIES AND BISCOTTI | serves 4 • time: 15 minutes

1 cup strawberries, hulled and halved
1 cup raspberries
1 cup blackberries
1 cup blueberries
1 cup powdered sugar
1 lemon, zested and juiced
3 cups good-quality ricotta cheese
   Store-bought almond biscotti

To prepare the mixed berries, combine the berries in a medium pot and place over low heat. Add ½ cup of the powdered sugar and lemon juice, then simmer for 7 to 10 minutes to allow the berries to macerate and break down slightly. Shut off the heat and set aside to cool while you prepare the ricotta.

To prepare the ricotta mixture, combine the remaining ½ cup powdered sugar, the lemon zest, and the ricotta in a food processor. Process until mixture is light and fluffy.

Spoon ricotta mixture into glasses and top with berry compote. Place biscotti on the side and serve.

12 / BABY IN THE KITCHEN

MENU

- ROASTED APPLES AND BLUEBERRIES
- BAKED SWEET POTATOES AND BANANAS
- BANANA BROWN RICE
- CREAMY CAULIFLOWER AND PARMESAN
- OATMEAL, ROASTED APPLE, AND CINNAMON
- ROASTED BUTTERNUT SQUASH WITH FRESH GINGER AND CINNAMON
- SWEET PEAS AND GREEN BEANS WITH MINT
- SUMMER SQUASH, ZUCCHINI, AND YUKON GOLD POTATOES
- CHICKEN NOODLE SOUP BABY-FRIENDLY VERSION
- SPAGHETTI BOLOGNESE BABY-FRIENDLY VERSION

A LOT OF YOU OUT THERE SEND ME EMAILS AND LETTERS THANKING ME FOR HELPING YOU FEED YOUR FAMILY IN NEW AND EXCITING WAYS. AND I CAN'T TELL YOU HOW MUCH I APPRECIATE IT.

I take your family's mealtime as seriously as I take my own. So when it came time to write this book, I tried to come up with a lot of variations of what dinner looks like at my place on any given day. Well, that usually involves my family, of course, so it would make sense to cook some meals for five, right? Yeah, if it were just that easy. Forty percent of my family only eats food that's been pureed in a blender!

A couple of years back, I began working on the idea of a baby food line called Sprout to fill a void I saw in the marketplace. When my son Miles was a baby, I worked really hard to learn all about the different stages of a baby's feeding because, frankly, I thought the baby food at the market tasted disgusting. I tested hundreds of recipes for flavor, texture, and age appropriateness to create a product that I am proud to put in the mouths of my own children.

Today I have three hungry kids at home, and they have no qualms about letting you know when they want to be fed. It would be easy to pop open that store-bought jar and feed some slop to them—in fact, they probably wouldn't complain. But you and I both know what tastes good and what doesn't, and, believe it or not, it really matters.

When babies are born, they are already developing a palate based on a diet of breast milk. After about six months of age, they begin to shift to solid foods. That's when most people turn to the supermarket shelves for their baby's menu. But most store-bought baby foods are highly processed and full of sugar, salt, and calories. And research has shown that when you feed your kids this type of diet, they will learn to seek salty and sweet foods and steer away from natural foods like fruits and vegetables flavored with herbs, spices, and other natural ingredients. On the other hand, give your children fresh, natural flavors and they won't want the processed stuff. Bad eating habits—which can lead to obesity, diabetes, and other health-related

problems—begin to develop as soon as your baby starts eating solid food. Don't we owe it to our kids to make decisions for them now that will help them make the best decisions for their health later?

In the recipes that follow, I've put together a range of flavors that Hayden really loves. He's old enough now to give me the heads-up on what's working for him and what just isn't doing it. Keep in mind that your baby might have different taste preferences than mine (isn't that the beauty of it), so try some of these out and see what flies. In my research, both academic and trial and error, I've realized that a really great way to get more flavor into my food without adding sugar is by roasting fruits and vegetables to bring out their natural sugars. The roasted foods have a much deeper flavor profile, and, in general, the consistency works better too. When you are putting together your own flavors, just use your palate for guidance. Unless, that is, jalapeño pepper puree sounds like a good idea. Oatmeal, apple, and cinnamon; sweet potato and banana—sounds good, right? It really is that easy, and it's really important.

When it comes time to sit down around the dinner table, let's not forget about our littlest diners and feed them something we wouldn't put in our own stomachs. You are their role models as they learn to make the right choices in their lives. What you put into their stomachs now will help them live healthier and happier lives as adults. I have a lot of fun cooking with my babies in the kitchen, and I hope you will too.

ROASTED APPLES AND BLUEBERRIES | approximately 3 cups • time: 35 minutes

4 large Golden Delicious apples
1 cup fresh blueberries

Preheat oven to 350°F. Cut the apples in half and remove cores. Set apples on a roasting tray, cut sides down, and bake in the preheated oven for 20 to 25 minutes, until they puff up. Add blueberries and bake for 5 minutes more. Remove from the oven. When cool enough to handle, remove apple skins. Puree apples and blueberries in a food processor until smooth. Immediately cool in the refrigerator.

BAKED SWEET POTATOES AND BANANAS | approximately 3 cups • time: 1 hour and 35 minutes

3 large sweet potatoes, unpeeled
2 bananas, unpeeled
Filtered water, as necessary

Preheat oven to 350°F. Pierce the skin of the sweet potatoes with a fork in several places. Place on a roasting tray and roast in the preheated oven for 1 hour. Add bananas and roast for 30 minutes more. Remove from the oven. When cool enough to handle, use a large spoon to scoop out the insides of the sweet potato and banana; discard skins. Combine sweet potato and banana in a food processor and puree until smooth, adding filtered water as necessary. Immediately cool in the refrigerator.

> **WHEN MILES WAS A BABY, I WORKED REALLY HARD TO LEARN ALL ABOUT THE DIFFERENT STAGES OF A BABY'S FEEDING BECAUSE, FRANKLY, I THOUGHT THAT THE BABY FOOD AT THE MARKET TASTED DISGUSTING.**

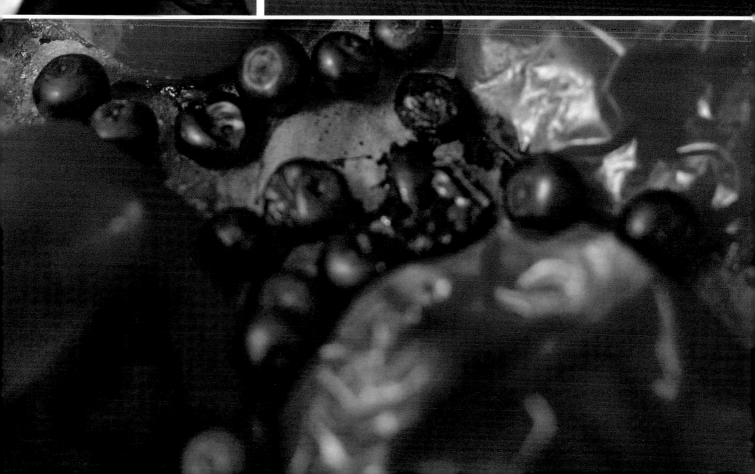

MOST STORE-BOUGHT BABY FOODS ARE HIGHLY PROCESSED AND FULL OF SUGAR, SALT, AND CALORIES.

CREAMY CAULIFLOWER AND PARMESAN (RECIPE, P. 196)

BANANA BROWN RICE | approximately 3 cups • time: 40 minutes

3 bananas, unpeeled
2 cups cooked brown rice
2 teaspoons ground cinnamon
   Filtered water, as necessary

Preheat oven to 350°F. Place bananas in their skins on a roasting tray and bake in the preheated oven for 30 minutes. Remove from the oven. When cool enough to handle, use a large scoop to remove insides of banana; discard skins. Puree banana in a food processor with brown rice and cinnamon until smooth, adding filtered water as necessary. Immediately cool in the refrigerator.

CREAMY CAULIFLOWER AND PARMESAN | approximately 2 cups • time: 15 minutes

1 medium head cauliflower
1 tablespoon unsalted butter (about 1 teaspoon
   per 8 ounces cauliflower)
1 tablespoon grated Parmesan (about 1 teaspoon
   per 8 ounces cauliflower)

Remove outer leaves of cauliflower and cut head into smaller pieces. Place in a pot with ½ inch water and set over medium heat. Simmer for 10 to 12 minutes, until tender. Remove from heat. Puree cauliflower with butter and Parmesan in a food processor until smooth. Immediately cool in the refrigerator.

"When it comes time to sit down around the dinner table, let's not forget about our littlest diners and feed them something we wouldn't put in our own stomachs. "

OATMEAL, ROASTED APPLE, AND CINNAMON | approximately 2 cups • time: 35 minutes

4 Golden Delicious apples
2 cups oatmeal (such as steel-cut or instant)
1 teaspoon ground cinnamon
Filtered water, as necessary

Preheat oven to 350°F. Cut the apples in half and remove cores. Set apples on a roasting tray, cut sides down, and bake in the preheated oven for 20 to 25 minutes, until they puff up. Remove from the oven. When apples are cool enough to handle, remove skins. Cook oatmeal in water according to package directions. Combine apples, oatmeal, and cinnamon in a food processor and puree until smooth, adding filtered water as necessary. Immediately cool in the refrigerator.

ROASTED BUTTERNUT SQUASH
WITH FRESH GINGER AND CINNAMON | approximately 2 cups • time: 45 minutes

1 medium butternut squash
1 small onion
1 tablespoon extra-virgin olive oil
1 tablespoon grated fresh ginger
1 teaspoon ground cinnamon

Preheat oven to 350°F. Cut squash in half and remove the seeds with a large spoon. Slice the onion into thick rings. Place squash, cut sides up, and onion on a roasting tray. Drizzle with olive oil and bake in the preheated oven about 35 minutes, until the tip of a knife goes in the squash without resistance (remove onion midway through, once caramelized). When cool enough to handle, remove flesh of squash with a large spoon. Combine squash, onion, ginger, and cinnamon in a food processor and puree until smooth. Immediately cool in the refrigerator.

SWEET PEAS AND GREEN BEANS
WITH MINT (RECIPE, P. 204)

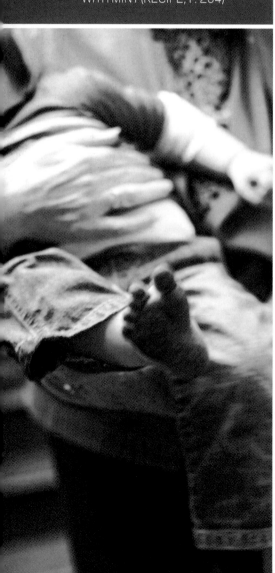

SWEET PEAS AND
GREEN BEANS WITH MINT

approximately 1½ cups • time: 12 minutes

1 cup shelled fresh peas
½ cup green beans, ends trimmed
1 fresh mint sprig, leaves only
Filtered water, as necessary

Combine peas, beans, and mint in a saucepan and add ¼ inch of water. Place over medium heat and simmer for 3 to 4 minutes, until beans are just tender. Drain vegetables and plunge into a large bowl of ice water to cool; drain. Place mixture in a food processor and puree until smooth. Immediately cool in the refrigerator.

SUMMER SQUASH,
ZUCCHINI, AND YUKON GOLD POTATOES

approximately 2 cups • time: 45 minutes

4 summer squash
2 zucchini
1 large Yukon gold potato
1 tablespoon extra-virgin olive oil
¼ cup grated Parmesan
Filtered water, as necessary

Preheat oven to 350°F. Pierce skins of the squash, zucchini, and potato with a fork in several places. Place on a roasting tray and drizzle with oil. Roast in the preheated oven for 25 to 35 minutes, until tender. Remove from the oven. Combine vegetables and Parmesan in the food processor and puree until smooth, adding filtered water as necessary. Immediately cool in the refrigerator.

> **THE ROASTED FOODS HAVE A MUCH DEEPER FLAVOR PROFILE, AND, IN GENERAL, THE CONSISTENCY WORKS BETTER TOO.**

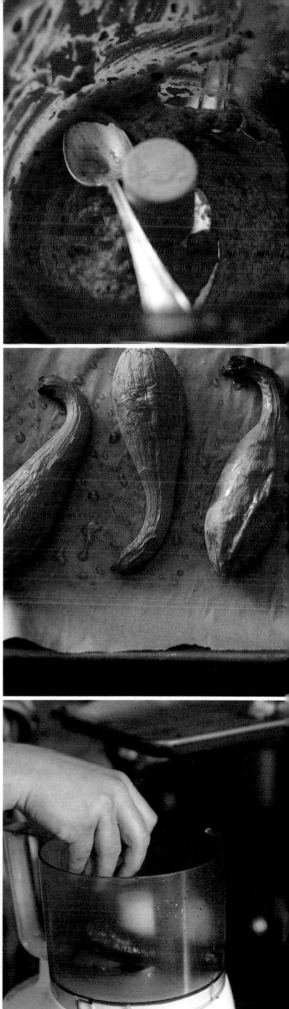

CHICKEN NOODLE SOUP
BABY-FRIENDLY VERSION

4 to 6 large servings • time: 45 minutes

1   store-bought deli roast chicken
2   quarts cold water
2   carrots, washed and sliced into circles
3   celery ribs, roughly chopped
1   small onion, chopped
2   garlic cloves, peeled and chopped
¼   bunch fresh thyme sprigs (4 sprigs), leaves only
    Kosher salt and freshly ground black pepper
2   cups dried pasta noodles
½   lemon, juice only
¼   bunch fresh parsley (about 4 sprigs), roughly chopped

Place the chicken in a large stockpot and add the water, carrot, celery, onion, garlic, and thyme. Place over medium heat and slowly bring to a boil to extract the flavors of the chicken. Reduce heat and simmer for 20 to 25 minutes, then remove chicken. Remove meat from chicken; shred meat. Discard skin and bones. Season chicken stock in pot with salt and pepper; add pasta and shredded meat. Bring soup to a boil, then reduce heat and simmer until pasta is cooked. Finish with lemon juice and parsley.

For adults, ladle soup into bowls and serve hot. For the baby-friendly version, allow a portion of the soup to cool. Puree cooled soup in a food processor until smooth.

SPAGHETTI BOLOGNESE

BABY-FRIENDLY VERSION

4 to 6 large servings • time: 1 hour 15 minutes

1   medium onion, roughly chopped
2   celery ribs, roughly chopped
2   carrots, peeled and roughly chopped
4   garlic cloves, peeled
    Extra-virgin olive oil
1   pound ground veal
1   pound ground beef
    Kosher salt and freshly ground black pepper
1   28-ounce can whole San Marzano tomatoes
1   cup milk
1   quart reduced-sodium chicken broth
2   teaspoons ground cinnamon
1   pound dried spaghetti
¼   cup grated Parmesan
¼   bunch fresh Italian flat-leaf parsley (about 4 sprigs), roughly chopped

Combine onion, celery, carrot, and garlic in a food processor. Puree until mixture is smooth and pulpy. Place a large pot over medium-high heat and add a 2-count of oil (about 2 tablespoons). Add vegetable pulp and cook for 3 to 4 minutes, until some of the moisture evaporates. Push vegetable pulp to the side and add ground veal and beef. Season well with salt and pepper. Cook until meat is nicely browned, breaking up the meat with the back of a wooden spoon as you cook. Hand-crush tomatoes and add to the pot along with tomato juices, milk, broth, and cinnamon. Bring to a boil, then reduce heat to low and simmer for 1 hour, until liquid has reduced and meat is tender. Taste and season with salt and pepper, if necessary.

Place a large pot of salted water over high heat and bring to a boil. Drop the spaghetti into the boiling water and cook until tender, yet firm (al dente). Drain well. Toss spaghetti in sauce and top with Parmesan and parsley.

For adults, portion Spaghetti Bolognese among bowls and serve hot. For the baby-friendly version, allow a portion of the mixture to cool. Place mixture in a food processor and pulse until noodles are roughly chopped.

13

SUNDAY NIGHT DINNER BY THE FIRE

Our Quality Standards

We carefully evaluate each and every product we sell.

We feature foods that are free from artificial preservatives, colors, flavors, sweeteners and hydrogenated fats.

We are passionate about great tasting food and the pleasure of sharing it with each other.

We are committed to foods that are fresh, wholesome and safe to eat.

We seek out

MENU

> BRAISED BEEF BRISKET
> PARSNIP PUREE
> RED ONIONS ROASTED WITH BALSAMIC AND HONEY
> ARBORIO RICE PUDDING WITH RUM-RAISIN MASCARPONE

THE CITY OF SAN FRANCISCO HAS AN AVERAGE YEARLY TEMPERATURE BELOW 60 DEGREES

I live just over the Golden Gate Bridge in a little town called Mill Valley, where it gets a bit warmer, but my house is tucked away in the woods beside a little creek. We're under a redwood canopy, which couldn't be more beautiful, but sometimes it seems to lock in that San Francisco chill and we start looking for a little bit of extra warmth. That gives us the perfect excuse to light up the fireplace and get that cozy vibe going.

At my place Sunday night is for relaxing. I'm on the road a lot, and when I finally get home, I have to scramble to catch up on the backlog of work. So come Sunday night, I do whatever I can to sit back, relax, and enjoy my family and our little place in the woods. Sundays are special for a lot of different reasons. People have their own traditions and routines—church, football, picnics, whatever. For me the fireside dinner is one of the best Sunday routines that I've been a part of, and I think this menu will help you see why. Fires are warm and enveloping, and I want my dishes to provide that same satisfying feeling. Call it comfort food, call it food for the soul, call it whatever you want. I just make what suits the mood and call it dinner!

In this case the mood calls for brisket—a tough cut of beef that is popular with many people for many dishes. It's brined for corned beef, it's a staple in traditional Jewish cooking, and it's second to none when it's smoked for barbeque. But no matter how you approach brisket, you've got to take it slow and cook it for quite a while to break down all of that tough connective tissue. I promise you, the flavor is well worth the wait.

For this meal I braise the brisket in red wine. The beef absorbs the rich flavors of the wine, herbs, vegetables, and seasonings and, in turn, also imparts heavy doses of its own flavor back into the broth. When it's finished, it's a savory, fork-tender masterpiece.

With this kind of heart-warming dish, you might expect mashed potatoes on the side. However, I prefer Parsnip Puree in this menu because you get that same smooth, creamy consistency but with a lighter and fresher flavor. Roast sweet red onions as a side dish and you have a full plate. Dessert continues down this smooth and satisfying path with an Arborio rice pudding that has a creamy consistency, similar to a sweet risotto.

You have a big week ahead of you, so on Sunday night it's time to relax. It doesn't matter whether you have a fireplace; just fill your stomach with this warm and comforting meal and you'll be ready to rock for another seven days.

BRAISED BEEF BRISKET | serves 10 • time: 3 hours 30 minutes

- 4 large garlic cloves, peeled and smashed
- ½ teaspoon kosher salt
- 4 fresh rosemary sprigs, needles stripped from the stem and chopped
- ¼ cup extra-virgin olive oil
- 1 4-pound beef brisket (first cut)
  Kosher salt and freshly ground black pepper
- 3 large carrots, cut into 3-inch chunks
- 3 ribs celery, cut into 3-inch chunks
- 2 onions, halved
- 2 cups dry red wine
- 1 16-ounce can whole tomatoes, hand-crushed
- 1 handful fresh Italian flat-leaf parsley
- 3 bay leaves
- 1 tablespoon all-purpose flour (optional)
- 2 tablespoons water or dry red wine (optional)
- 1 bunch hydroponic watercress, for garnish (optional)
- 1 recipe Parsnip Puree (see recipe, page 219)

Preheat oven to 325°F. On a cutting board, mash the garlic and ½ teaspoon salt together with the flat side of a knife until it turns into a paste. Add the rosemary and continue to mash until incorporated. Put the garlic-rosemary paste in a small bowl and add 2 tablespoons of the oil; stir to combine. Set aside.

Season both sides of the brisket with plenty of salt and pepper. Rub the rosemary-garlic paste over the brisket. Drizzle with additional olive oil. Place a large roasting pan or Dutch oven over medium-high heat. When the pan is hot, place the brisket in the roasting pan and sear to form a nice brown crust on both sides, adding additional oil as necessary to prevent sticking. Lay the vegetables all around the brisket. Add the wine, tomatoes, tomato liquid, parsley, and bay leaves. Cover the pan tightly with a lid or aluminum foil and bake in the preheated oven for 3 to 4 hours, basting every 30 minutes with the pan juices, until the beef is fork-tender.

Remove the brisket from pan and place on a cutting board. Allow brisket to rest for 15 minutes. Remove vegetables from the pan with a slotted spoon; discard vegetables. Skim some of the excess fat from the pan juices, leaving about ¼ cup fat in the pan; place the roasting pan with the pan juices and fat over medium-high heat. Boil and stir about 5 minutes, until the sauce is reduced by half. (For a thicker sauce, mix the 1 tablespoon flour with the 2 tablespoons water and whisk into the gravy.) Slice brisket and serve with sauce over Parsnip Puree. If you like, garnish each plate with watercress.

"For me, the fireside dinner is one of the best Sunday routines that I've been a part of, and I think this menu will help you see why."

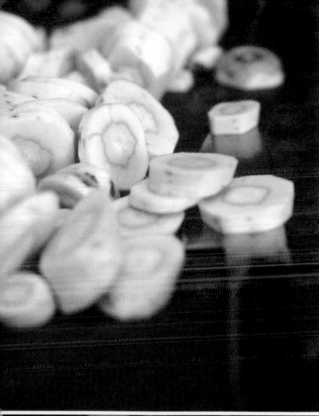

PARSNIP PUREE | serves 4 to 6 • time: 35 minutes

1 pound parsnips, peeled and sliced
   Kosher salt
4 garlic cloves
1 thyme sprig
1 cup milk
1 cup heavy whipping cream
1 stick unsalted butter, cut into pieces
   Freshly ground black pepper
   Extra-virgin olive oil

Put parsnips in a pot, season with salt, and add garlic and thyme. Cover with the milk and cream. Place pot over medium heat and bring to a simmer. Simmer for 12 to 15 minutes, until tender (the tip of a paring knife should go through parsnip pieces without resistance). Drain parsnips and reserve cooking liquid. Place parsnips in a food processor with butter. Process and add enough of reserved cooking liquid to achieve texture of whipped cream. Season to taste with salt and additional pepper and finish with a drizzle of oil.

RED ONIONS ROASTED WITH BALSAMIC AND HONEY | serves 4 to 6 • time: 45 minutes

¼ cup extra-virgin olive oil
2 tablespoons balsamic vinegar
⅓ cup honey
½ bunch fresh thyme sprigs (about 8 sprigs), leaves only
   Kosher salt and freshly ground black pepper
3 red onions, halved and papery outer peel removed
3 tablespoons unsalted butter, cut into 6 slices
   Fresh thyme sprigs

Preheat oven to 375°F. Whisk together the oil, vinegar, honey, and thyme. Season with salt and pepper; whisk until combined. Put the onions in a large bowl and pour the dressing over them. Toss together until the onions are coated. Put the onions on a roasting tray, cut sides up, and drizzle with additional vinegar. Top each onion half with a butter slice and thyme sprig. Roast in the preheated oven about 40 minutes, until the onions are soft and slightly caramelized.

CALL IT COMFORT FOOD, CALL IT FOOD FOR THE SOUL, CALL IT WHATEVER YOU WANT. I JUST MAKE WHAT SUITS THE MOOD AND CALL IT DINNER!

ARBORIO RICE PUDDING
WITH RUM-RAISIN MASCARPONE

serves 4 • time: 45 minutes

Rum-Raisin Mascarpone
1 cup raisins, packed tightly
1 cup sugar
½ cup dark rum
1 lemon, juice only
2 cups mascarpone cheese
2 cups heavy whipping cream

Pudding
3 cups whole milk
2 tablespoons unsalted butter
1 cup packed light brown sugar
½ teaspoon ground cinnamon
1 vanilla bean, split and scraped
1 cup Arborio rice
Pinch kosher salt
½ cup crème fraîche
Lemon zest

To prepare Rum-Raisin Mascarpone, soak raisins in a mixture of the granulated sugar, rum, and lemon juice. Muddle (squash) raisins with a wooden spoon to help them soak and rehydrate a little. Set aside while you prepare the rice pudding.

Put milk, butter, brown sugar, cinnamon, vanilla bean contents, rice, and salt into a large saucepan. Bring to a simmer over medium heat; stirring constantly. Simmer Arborio rice for 20 to 22 minutes, until tender, yet firm (al dente). (The rice mixture should have slightly more liquid than regular risotto.) Remove from heat; stir in crème fraîche.

Strain the liquid from the raisins; reserve liquid. Combine mascarpone and cream and whisk until light and creamy in a large bowl. Swirl in the strained raisins and drizzle a little of the soaking liquid over top. Garnish rice pudding with lemon zest. Top rice pudding with a generous spoonful of Rum-Raisin Mascarpone. Serve pudding with additional Rum-Raisin Mascarpone on the side.

14

CHEAT SHEET

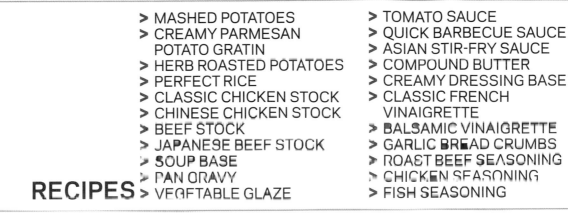

RECIPES

- MASHED POTATOES
- CREAMY PARMESAN POTATO GRATIN
- HERB ROASTED POTATOES
- PERFECT RICE
- CLASSIC CHICKEN STOCK
- CHINESE CHICKEN STOCK
- BEEF STOCK
- JAPANESE BEEF STOCK
- SOUP BASE
- PAN GRAVY
- VEGETABLE GLAZE

- TOMATO SAUCE
- QUICK BARBECUE SAUCE
- ASIAN STIR-FRY SAUCE
- COMPOUND BUTTER
- CREAMY DRESSING BASE
- CLASSIC FRENCH VINAIGRETTE
- BALSAMIC VINAIGRETTE
- GARLIC BREAD CRUMBS
- ROAST BEEF SEASONING
- CHICKEN SEASONING
- FISH SEASONING

I'VE CREATED THIS "CHEAT SHEET" TO GIVE YOU SOME STANDBY RECIPES AND IDEAS that you can build into your repertoire at a moment's notice. Feel free to mix and match these recipes with any of the scenarios that I've laid out in this book, and by all means, treat them as inspirations and building blocks for more ideas!

MASHED POTATOES | serves 4 to 6 • time: 30 minutes

- 1 cup heavy whipping cream
- ½ stick unsalted butter
- 4 large Yukon gold potatoes, peeled
  Kosher salt and freshly ground black pepper
- ¼ cup extra-virgin olive oil

Combine cream and butter in a small saucepan and place over medium heat. Heat until butter melts; set aside.

Place the potatoes in a medium saucepan. Add enough cold water to cover potatoes and place over high heat. Bring to boil, then add 1 teaspoon of salt and reduce heat to a simmer. Simmer for 15 to 20 minutes, until the potatoes are very tender. Drain. Pass the potatoes through a food mill or ricer into a large bowl. Stir in the warm cream mixture until the cream mixture is absorbed and the potatoes are smooth. Season the potatoes with salt and pepper and finish them off by stirring in oil.

CREAMY PARMESAN POTATO GRATIN | serves 4 to 6 • time: 1 hour

- 1½ cups heavy whipping cream
- 1 fresh thyme sprig
- 2 garlic cloves, peeled and chopped
- ½ teaspoon ground nutmeg
- 1 tablespoon unsalted butter
- 2 pounds russet potatoes, peeled and cut into ⅛-inch-thick slices
  Kosher salt and freshly ground black pepper
- ½ cup grated Parmesan, plus more for broiling

Preheat the oven to 375°F. Combine cream, thyme, garlic, and nutmeg in a small saucepan. Place saucepan over medium heat and cook until cream is heated. While cream is heating, butter a 13×8-inch casserole dish. Place a layer of potato in an overlapping pattern and season with salt and pepper. Remove cream mixture from heat; discard thyme sprig. Pour about one-third of the cream mixture over the potatoes. Top with one-third of the ½ cup grated Parmesan. Make two more layers with potatoes, cream mixture, and cheese. Bake, uncovered, in the preheated oven for 45 minutes. Sprinkle with some additional Parmesan and broil about 5 minutes, until cheese browns.

HERB ROASTED POTATOES | serves 4 to 6 • time: 1 hour 10 minutes

6   large Yukon gold potatoes
     Extra-virgin olive oil
4   fresh rosemary sprigs
1   garlic head, cut in half through the equator (horizontally)
     Kosher salt and freshly ground black pepper

Preheat oven to 350°F. Place a roasting tray in the oven so it can
heat up. Wash potatoes and cut them into ¾-inch pieces.

Once the roasting tray is hot, remove tray from oven and drizzle with
oil (this creates a nonstick surface so your potatoes won't stick to the
tray). Add potatoes and top with rosemary and garlic. Season with salt
and pepper then roast for 1 hour until crispy and golden.

PERFECT RICE | makes 2½ cups • time: 18 minutes

2   cups long grain white rice
4   cups water

Combine rice and water in a medium saucepan and place over high
heat. Bring to a boil and reduce to a simmer. Simmer, covered,
for 12 minutes. When done, remove lid and fluff with a fork.

CLASSIC CHICKEN STOCK | makes 2 quarts • time: 1 hour 15 minutes

2   carrots, cut into large chunks
2   ribs celery, cut into large chunks
2   large white onions, quartered
1   turnip, halved
1   head of garlic, cut in half through the equator (horizontally)
1   3½-pound certified organic chicken, cleaned and rinsed
¼   bunch fresh thyme sprigs (about 4 sprigs)
2   bay leaves
1   teaspoon whole black peppercorns

Combine the vegetables, garlic, and chicken in a large stockpot. Pour in enough cold water to just cover the bird (about 3 quarts). Place pot over medium heat. Toss in the thyme, bay leaves, and peppercorns and slowly bring the liquid to a boil. Once liquid is boiling, lower the heat to medium-low and gently simmer for 1 hour, partially covered, until the chicken is cooked through. As it cooks, skim off any foam and impurities that rise to the surface. (Add more water, if necessary, to keep the chicken covered while simmering.) Place chicken on a cutting board. When it's cool enough to handle, clean the meat from bones; discard skin and bones. Shred the meat; place in a container for later use. Strain stock through a fine sieve into another pot to remove the vegetables. Cover stock; refrigerate for up to 1 week or freeze.

CHINESE CHICKEN STOCK | makes 2 quarts • time: 1 hour 15 minutes

2   red chiles, whole
4   green onions, whole
4   fresh cilantro sprigs
6   dried shiitake mushrooms
2   1-inch pieces ginger, peeled and sliced
6   whole black peppercorns
1   head of garlic, cut in half through the equator (horizontally)
¼   cup soy sauce
1   3½-pound certified organic chicken, cleaned and rinsed

Combine all ingredients in a large stockpot. Pour in enough cold water to just cover the bird (about 3 quarts). Place pot over medium heat and allow it to slowly come to a boil. Once the liquid is boiling, lower the heat to medium-low and gently simmer for 1 hour, partially covered, until the chicken is cooked through. As it cooks, skim off any foam and impurities that rise to the surface. (Add more water, if necessary, to keep the chicken covered while simmering.) Place chicken on a cutting board. When it's cool enough to handle, clean the meat from bones; discard skin and bones. Shred the meat; place in a container for later use. Strain stock through a fine sieve into another pot to remove the vegetables. Cover stock; refrigerate for up to 1 week or freeze.

BEEF STOCK | makes 2 quarts • time: 6 hours

5   pounds beef bones, sawed into pieces (have your butcher do this)
    Extra-virgin olive oil
2   medium onions, quartered
4   ribs celery, cut into large pieces
2   large carrots, cut into large pieces
1   head of garlic, cut in half through the equator (horizontally)
½   bunch thyme (about 8 sprigs)
1   750-milliliter bottle dry red wine
1   tablespoon black peppercorns
1   bunch fresh parsley stems (about 16 stems)
4   bay leaves
    Kosher salt

Preheat the oven to 400°F. Place the bones in a roasting pan and drizzle with olive oil. Roast in the preheated oven for 1 hour. Remove from oven and place the vegetables, garlic, and thyme over the bones and continue to roast for 30 minutes. Remove from oven and scrape the bones and vegetables into a large stockpot.

Place the roasting pan over high heat on the stovetop and add the wine to the hot pan. Deglaze the pan by scraping the bottom to release the brown bits (sucs). Add this deglazed liquid to the pot along with peppercorns, parsley stems, and bay leaves. Season lightly with salt. Bring to a boil and reduce to a simmer. Simmer for 4 hours, skimming any foam, impurities, and fat that rise to the surface. Strain the stock through a fine sieve into another pot to remove the solids. Cover stock; refrigerate for up to 1 week or freeze.

JAPANESE BEEF BROTH | makes 2 quarts • time: 1 hour 15 minutes

2   quarts reduced-sodium beef broth
¼   cup low-sodium soy sauce
6   dried shiitake mushrooms
1   sheet kombu (dried seaweed)
2   tablespoons sugar
2   1-inch pieces ginger, peeled and sliced
1½   cups 1-inch slices green onion
8   ounces thinly sliced beef tenderloin

Combine all the ingredients, except green onion and tenderloin, in a large stockpot. Place pot over high heat and bring to a boil. Reduce heat to a simmer and simmer, covered, for 1 hour. Remove kombu and ginger. Add green onion and beef and simmer for about 2 to 3 minutes, until beef is just cooked. Serve with cooked noodles (such as udon or ramen noodles) or use as a base for other recipes.

SOUP BASE | makes 2 quarts • time: 45 minutes

½   stick unsalted butter
3   tablespoons all-purpose flour
6   cups reduced-sodium chicken broth, heated
2   garlic cloves, gently smashed
1   bay leaf
1   small onion, thinly sliced

4   cups desired vegetables (such as watercress, broccoli, cauliflower, peas, or asparagus)
   Kosher salt and freshly ground black pepper

To make the soup base, in a medium saucepan melt butter over medium heat. Add flour and stir until combined. Continue to cook about 5 minutes, until just golden. Slowly add chicken broth. Add garlic, bay leaf, and onion. Simmer for 12 minutes. To the soup base, add desired vegetables and cook until tender (time will depend on what vegetables you choose). Remove bay leaf. Season lightly with salt and pepper. Carefully puree mixture in small batches in a blender until silky smooth. (When pureeing hot foods, hold a towel firmly over the lid of the blender cover.) Season to taste and serve.

PAN GRAVY | makes 3 cups • time: 20 minutes

1 large onion, roughly chopped
1 medium carrot, cut into chunks
2 ribs celery, cut into chunks
2 fresh thyme sprigs
2 cups dry red or white wine
4 cups beef or chicken broth
1 tablespoon unsalted butter, softened
1 tablespoon all-purpose flour
    Kosher salt and freshly ground black pepper

After you have roasted the meat of your choice, pour any pan juices into a degreasing cup. Pour off fat, reserving 2 tablespoons and discarding the rest. Set aside the defatted pan juices. Set the roasting pan over high heat and add the reserved 2 tablespoons fat. Sauté onion, carrot, celery, and thyme for 3 to 5 minutes, until vegetables are tender. Add wine (use red if your roast is red meat and white if your roast is white) to hot pan. Deglaze the pan by scraping the bottom to release the brown bits (sucs). Add broth (use beef broth if your roast is red meat; chicken broth if your roast is white) and reserved pan juices. Simmer for 10 to 12 minutes. Meanwhile, make a paste by thoroughly combining butter and flour in a small bowl. Add paste to the liquid in the pan as you whisk. Simmer until gravy thickens; season with salt and pepper. Strain gravy and serve.

VEGETABLE GLAZE | makes 4 servings• time: 10 minutes

1 tablespoon unsalted butter
1 tablespoon extra-virgin olive oil
4 cup desired vegetables, trimmed and cleaned
    Reduced-sodium chicken broth
    Kosher salt and freshly ground black pepper

Place a sauté pan over medium-high heat and add butter and olive oil. Add trimmed, cleaned vegetables and sauté for 5 to 7 minutes, until tender (timing depends on the size and type of vegetables). Add a splash of chicken broth and season with salt and pepper. Toss to coat vegetables and serve.

TOMATO SAUCE | makes 4 cups • time: 35 minutes

Extra-virgin olive oil
1 garlic clove, minced
1 small onion, diced
1 28-ounce can whole San Marzano tomatoes, undrained
1 tablespoon torn fresh basil leaves
Kosher salt and freshly ground black pepper
1 teaspoon sugar

Set a medium saucepan over medium heat and add a 2-count of oil (about 2 tablespoons). Add garlic and onion and sauté until fragrant and translucent. Add tomatoes with their juice and basil. Use a wooden spoon to break up tomatoes. Season with salt and pepper. Stir in sugar. Cover and simmer for 20 to 25 minutes.

QUICK BARBECUE SAUCE | makes about 3 cups • time: 35 minutes

Extra-virgin olive oil
½ onion, sliced
2 garlic cloves, gently smashed
2 cups ketchup
¼ cup packed brown sugar
¼ cup molasses
2 tablespoons red wine vinegar
1 tablespoon dry mustard
1 teaspoon ground cumin
1 teaspoon ground paprika
Kosher salt and freshly ground black pepper

Set a large saucepan over medium heat and add a 2-count of oil (about 2 tablespoons). Add the onion and garlic and cook slowly over medium-low heat without caramelizing for 5 minutes, stirring often. Add the remaining sauce ingredients, except the salt and pepper. Stir to mix. Simmer for 20 minutes to allow the flavors to come together. Season with salt and plenty of pepper. Using a slotted spoon, remove onion and garlic. Cool sauce and serve.

ASIAN STIR-FRY SAUCE
makes 2 cups • time: 20 minutes

Peanut oil
1 tablespoon grated fresh ginger
2 garlic cloves, minced
1 tablespoon hoisin sauce
⅓ cup reduced-sodium soy sauce
⅔ cup packed brown sugar
1 cup reduced-sodium beef broth
1 small fresh red chile, finely sliced (add desired amount for heat) (see tip, page 60)
1 heaping tablespoon cornstarch
1 tablespoon water

Set a small saucepan over medium heat and add a 2-count of oil (about 2 tablespoons). Add ginger and garlic and sauté until fragrant. Add hoisin, soy sauce, brown sugar, broth, and desired amount of sliced chile.

Reduce heat and simmer about 15 minutes, until slightly syrupy. Combine cornstarch and water in a small bowl, then slowly add to the sauce while stirring. Remove from heat when sauce has thickened. Toss with stir-fried vegetables and/or meat.

COMPOUND BUTTER
makes 1 cup • time: 12 minutes

2 sticks unsalted butter, room temperature
4 garlic cloves, peeled and minced
1 handful fresh Italian flat-leaf parsley
Kosher salt and freshly ground black pepper

Combine ingredients in a food processor and process until well combined. Shape butter mixture into a log on a large sheet of parchment paper. Roll the log up in the parchment paper and twist the ends of the paper. Store in the refrigerator. To use, slice off disks; remove paper. Use on top of steaks, bread, or vegetables.

NOTE You can use a variety of ingredients for different flavor profiles in your compound butter, such as roasted cashews, sun-dried tomatoes, basil, or chives.

CREAMY DRESSING BASE | makes 1 cup • time: 5 minutes

½ cup sour cream
½ cup store-bought mayonnaise
1 teaspoon lemon juice
   Kosher salt and freshly ground black pepper
   Desired add-ins (such as chopped fresh herbs or roasted garlic)

To make the dressing base, combine sour cream, mayonnaise, lemon juice, salt, and pepper in a medium bowl and stir to combine. Stir in desired add-ins for extra flavor.

CLASSIC FRENCH VINAIGRETTE | makes ¾ cup • time: 8 minutes

1 small shallot, finely diced
2 teaspoons Dijon mustard
2 tablespoons red wine vinegar
½ cup extra-virgin olive oil
   Kosher salt and freshly ground black pepper
1 tablespoon chopped fresh herb (parsley, tarragon, or chives) (optional)

Combine shallot, mustard, and vinegar in a mixing bowl. While constantly whisking, add oil in a slow, steady stream until the vinaigrette emulsifies. Once all the oil has been added and the vinaigrette has emulsified, season with salt and pepper. If you like, stir in herb.

BALSAMIC VINAIGRETTE | makes ¾ cup • time: 10 minutes

1   small shallot, finely diced
¼   cup finely chopped fresh Italian flat-leaf parsley
1   tablespoon Dijon mustard
2   tablespoons balsamic vinegar
1   tablespoon sugar
¾   cup extra-virgin olive oil
    Kosher salt and freshly ground black pepper

Combine shallot, parsley, mustard, vinegar, and sugar in a mixing
bowl. While constantly whisking, add oil in a slow, steady stream until
the vinaigrette emulsifies. Once all the oil has been added and the
vinaigrette has emulsified, season with salt and pepper.

GARLIC BREAD CRUMBS | makes 2 cups • time: 12 minutes

2   cups panko bread crumbs
2   garlic cloves, peeled and minced
1   handful fresh Italian flat-leaf parsley
    Kosher salt and freshly ground black pepper
¼   cup extra-virgin olive oil

Combine bread crumbs, garlic, and parsley in a large bowl and stir to
combine. Season well with salt and pepper and moisten with olive oil.
Sprinkle liberally on gratins or roasts and cook as you would normally.
Or bake in a roasting tray in a 350°F oven for 7 to 8 minutes, until
golden and crispy, and sprinkle on finished dishes such as fish
or vegetables.

ROAST BEEF SEASONING | makes ¾ cup • time: 7 minutes

1½ cups (about 2 ounces) dried porcini mushrooms
1 tablespoon garlic powder
½ bunch fresh thyme sprigs (about 8 sprigs), leaves only
Kosher salt and freshly ground black pepper

Combine ingredients in a blender and process until you have a fine powder. To use on beef, rub olive oil all over the roast and sprinkle with the seasoning. Roast beef as you would normally.

CHICKEN SEASONING | makes ¼ cup • time: 3 minutes

2 tablespoons ground dried sage
2 tablespoons ground celery seed
Kosher salt and freshly ground black pepper

Combine ingredients in a small bowl. To use, sprinkle liberally on chicken. Roast or grill chicken as you would normally.

FISH SEASONING | makes ¼ cup • time: 5 minutes

1 teaspoon lemon zest
2 tablespoons ground toasted fennel seeds
1 tablespoon fresh thyme leaves, chopped
1 tablespoon fresh marjoram leaves, chopped
Kosher salt and freshly ground black pepper

Combine all ingredients in a small bowl. To use, sprinkle liberally on fish. Grill or bake fish as you would normally.

ACKNOWLEDGMENTS

AFTER ALMOST 13 YEARS IN MANHATTAN, I MOVED MY FAMILY TO CALIFORNIA IN 2007 AND BOUGHT MY FIRST REAL HOUSE.

In the middle of moving in, with boxes piled up to the ceiling and a remodeling crew in residence, there was one thing you could always count on—I was cooking on a regular basis, no matter how much dust, debris, and paint fumes surrounded me. I was inspired by Northern California and the areas around our home, from the amazing coastal farms over the hills in Bolinas to the local Marin County Farmers Market to my own backyard in Mill Valley, where plums and blackberries grow wild. I knew I had found the perfect place to expand myself as a chef and for my family to put down roots.

Somehow, in the midst of the madness of relocating, my wife, Tolan, had the thought to keep a notebook handy and record memorable meals that we had enjoyed at home. When the time came to write my next cookbook, I spent a few days wracking my brain for something new and fresh. When I finally hit a wall, she took the binder out of a drawer and handed it to me. I instantly realized that this book had practically written itself.

There are so many wonderful people for me to thank. Starting with my right-hand man and the person that I refer to as "my main man Tony"—Anthony Hoy Fong. Not only is he the culinary director for my company, he's also my friend and constant companion in the kitchen and wherever our travels take us. He is the most buttoned-up guy that I have ever had the pleasure to work with. I would not be able to have such masterfully tested and accurate recipes without all of his hard work. Also, my Director of Operations Reid Strathearn—another class act who is a constant in my life. Reid is always willing and able to help out in any way he can. My thanks to you both.

Kevin Crafts—food stylist extraordinaire—your energy and attention to detail are always spot on and you are a pleasure to work with. And a special thank you to Victoria, Penny, Wes, Rochelle, and Erin for all of the help in the kitchen and making the food and ingredients look so great.

I met Squire Fox, the photographer who shot this book, when he came to New York to shoot me for the cover of *Charleston* magazine. We instantly hit it off and formed a friendship. Years later he shot my wedding, and when it came time to shoot this book he was the perfect guy for the job. A very special thanks to his assistant Sully, who may be one of the funniest guys I have ever met. Waking up and getting to work with this team every day in my home was hysterical. What a blast we all had!

For the props, the styling, and their constant staging and reorganizing of my house and kitchen, I owe a huge thank you to my mother-in-law Marjorie Clark and Tolan's godmother Janet Mercer Cohen. Together with my wife they scoured flea markets, eBay, estate sales, and antique fairs, building a prop room in our home that was fit for a king. That room was my one-stop shopping place for every plate, dish, linen, and piece of cutlery seen in this book.

I am proud to say that almost all of the ingredients we used in the making of this book were purchased less than a mile away from my house at one of the greatest neighborhood markets I have ever known, The Mill Valley Market. Thank you to the Canepa family and to their kind staff, who always helped us find the finest products and local purveyors.

And last but certainly not least, thank you to my family. My wife, Tolan, my sons Miles and Hayden, my daughter Dorothy (the first Florence girl), our dogs Jake and Eddie, and Eugene the deer, who lives in our backyard. There would be no place worth having dinner without all of you there with me. I love you.

Also, to all of the amazing vendors that I have the good fortune of working with and experiencing their brands firsthand—Viking and the people at the Gene Schick Company sent the top-of-the-line equipment and appliances that you see in my kitchen. I cannot say enough about the Viking line of products … thank you. To my friends at Heath Ceramics, I love your dishes and I love your tile. Few companies make it the old-fashioned way anymore, and I am lucky enough to live a few miles away from your headquarters and factory. Thank you for the constant supply of tile samples and for sending over so many of your handcrafted pieces that appear in this book. I would also like to thank Wüsthof, LamsonSharp knives, All-Clad cookware, Mauviel cookware, Ruffoni Italian copper cookware, Falk, Proteak cutting boards from sustainable forests, Anchor Hocking, Golden Gate Meat Company, Cowgirl Creamery, Hog Island Oyster Company, Fish in Sausalito, Whole Foods, McEvoy Olive Oil, Mikasa, Dean & DeLuca, Ozark West, Shun, and Outset.

INDEX

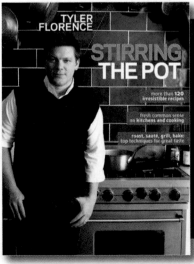

MASTER MEALTIME WITH TYLER FLORENCE *STIRRING THE POT*

A hands-on guide to help readers fall in love with their kitchen all over again.

Tyler teaches you how to set yourself up for success by stocking and organizing your kitchen like a pro.

More than 100 recipes you can master with confidence.

Loaded with photos, including one of every recipe.

Available where all great books are sold!